Dear Reader,

Before I became interested in dog behaviour, I had various problems with my own reactive dogs ... and through a lack of knowledge I often exacerbated their problems.

After discovering how to aid my own dogs I now work self-employed as the Yorkshire Dog Whisperer. I enjoy helping others to avoid the pitfalls that I myself fell into.

I teach people how to communicate a message to their dogs. This includes positive reinforcement, using your energy and body language to disagreeing with your dog ... yet does not necessitate being excessively dominant.

If you find Communicate A Message - Transform Behaviour to be helpful please let others know by leaving a review on Amazon.

Many thanks,

Nicky

DEDICATION

I wish to dedicate this book to my Grandad (Ken Adams) a humble yet great man whom I inherited my love of dogs from. I was privileged that his border collie trusted me enough to go onoff lead walks with me. She was very discerning and would only go for a walk with my Grandad, my Uncle and me.

With my Grandad and his collie Kina.

VIDEO LINKS

All videos can be found on Dailymotion (a video-sharing site similar to YouTube). Search for Yorkshire Dog Whisperer and select CHANNELS (NOT Videos or Playlists), before selecting ALL VIDEOS. This ensures you have access to all the videos (over 30) to accompany this book in one place.

CLIENT REVIEWS

"Had a one to one with Nicky today, found it very helpful not only for my dog, but (for) myself as well."

"I've been a police dog handler for a number of years, but after 60 minutes with Nicky I learnt so much and can say that the hour I spent with her was eye opening.

"Thank you so much Nicky. Rio is a completely different dog now to before you came. He's so much more relaxed. People have even been asking me for advice. You really have made things so much easier for us."

"Nicky was great and our dog has improved after our 1-1 session. The session helped my confidence too."

CLIENT QUESTIONNAIRES

I always ask my clients to fill in a questionnaire at the start of a session. The questionnaire includes any unwanted behaviour their dog exhibits. However, perhaps the most important question on the form concerns the owner:

OWNER'S EMOTIONS WHEN THE BEHAVIOUR OCCURS?

If you are reading this book because you have a specific behavioural problem you want help with, then please just take a minute to think about what emotions you experience when your dog displays this behaviour.

If you are getting angry, frustrated or anxious then join the club … in the past I experienced all of these emotions! But hopefully by the time you reach the end of this book, you will realise why these emotions are only exacerbating your dog's problems and have learned how to communicate the correct message.

TABLE OF CONTENTS

PART ONE - COMMUNICATE A MESSAGE

1. Dog Communication — Page 9
2. Communication Tools — Page 23
3. Nature and Nurture — Page 30

PART TWO - PREVENTION AND CURE FOR BEHAVIOURAL PROBLEMS

1. Pulling on the Lead — Page 34
2. Dogs who won't Walk on the Lead/ use the Stairs/Jump into a Car — Page 48
3. Dog Reactive Dogs — Page 51
4. Traffic Reactive Dogs — Page 80
5. People Reactive Dogs — Page 82
6. Child Reactive Dogs — Page 99
7. Cat/Small Pet Reactive Dogs — Page 104
8. Nipping — Page 110
9. Food and Toy Guarding — Page 113
10. Fussy Eaters — Page 119
11. Stealing Food — Page 121
12. Stealing Objects — Page 117
13. General Anxiety and Fireworks — Page 128
14. Separation Anxiety — Page 131
15. Poor Travellers — Page 138

16. Excessive Barking   Page 143
17. Jumping Up   Page 153
18. Stalking Lawn Mowers,
Vacuum Cleaners etc   Page 160
19. Hyperactive/Obsessive Dogs   Page 163
20. Poor Recall   Page 168
21. Toilet Training   Page 179
22. Crate Training   Page 181

PART THREE - USEFUL COMMANDS

1. Voice Control   Page 185
2. Intention   Page 187
3. Hand-signals   Page 188
4. Sit   Page 189
5. Leave It   Page 190
6. Wait   Page 192
7. Go Play   Page 194
8. Bed   Page 195

PART ONE

COMMUNICATE A MESSAGE

1. DOG COMMUNICATION

To communicate the right message to your dog you need to have an understanding of how they perceive and interact within the world. The two key factors dogs relate to are **energy** and **body language**. To dogs unless your energy is expressed in your spoken word or a learned command phrase then English is an unknown language.

ENERGY

Dogs like most animals react instinctively to different energy intensities. Your dog doesn't judge you on your appearance, they see you as energy and respond accordingly to the energy you are transmitting.

You might not be aware that your emotions are affecting the energy you are emitting to communicate with your dog, but either consciously or unconsciously your body is always having a conversation with your canine friend.

Our bodies produce electricity and are surrounded by an electromagnetic field, changes in which your dog can identify. In order to communicate with your dog, and get them to behave as you want you need to be aware of the messages you are sending them.

In my footloose and single days (pre-husband and children) I was a globe-trotting windsurf instructor. On my travels I learned the technique of telling an engaging story to help my students retain more information. So to grab your attention, and hopefully to ensure you remember this key principle the following story involves a **nudist beach!**

CASE STUDY - KEY PRINCIPLE

Whilst living in Cyprus in my twenties I rescued a gorgeous pointer cross who was generally a very happy go lucky, friendly dog. I was very close to Eddie ... living alone at the time ... for me Eddie was my family and constant companion.

Eddie never showed any aggression towards other dogs, despite being attacked on various occasions by a few Cypriot dogs, and he only once showed any signs of aggression towards people.

I encountered the people in question on an isolated and deserted cliff top which unbeknownst to me was near to a nudist beach! With no other people in sight my feelings of ANXIETY increased as two old men walked towards me brandishing walking sticks, walking boots and great all over body tans! Eddie was off the lead, but picked up on my unease and for the one and only time took on the role of protector. He instinctively issued a low warning growl and raised his hackles.

I had unconsciously given him the instructions through my lack of confidence "don't trust these people". Your relationship with your dog is founded on TRUST, LOVE and RESPECT – so my lack of trust in the naked old men caused my dog to mistrust them too.

Eddie on the clifftop near the nudist beach in Cyprus.

As I've established dogs respond and read your energy, so in order to communicate with your dog you need to be aware of the signals you are emitting. Your varying **positive energy** levels - calm, excited or confident - can be used to great effect to help relay the right instructions to your dog. They can be employed in different circumstances at critical times to communicate in essence what can be broken down as instructions.

POSITIVE EMOTIONS THAT CAN HELP YOUR DOG

- **CONFIDENCE**
- **CALMNESS**
- **EXCITEMENT**

You also need to be aware that **negative energy** such as anxiety, embarrassment or anger can convey the wrong message to your dog and result in unwanted behaviour. A lack of confidence when you are feeling unsure can translate to your dog feeling unsure and reacting accordingly. In the case of ANGER it can sometimes increase the intensity of the situation, and make your dog react more – as with an excited jumpy dog, or a barking dog.

NEGATIVE EMOTIONS THAT CAN PRODUCE UNWANTED BEHAVIOUR

- **ANXIETY**
- **FEAR**
- **ANGER**
- **FRUSTRATION**
- **GUILT**
- **EMBARRASSMENT**
- **PITY**

That's not to say you shouldn't ever feel sorry for your dog, but rather if you express this emotion you might not be helping your dog to build their own confidence and overcome a behavioural problem.

In the case of reactive dogs the wrong emotions in certain situations can add fuel to the fire.

Reactive Dog + Negatively Emotional Human = Explosive Situation

Reactive Dog + Calm Confident Human = Less Reactive Situation

If you continue to try to communicate with your dog verbally ("don't do that" or "it's okay baby") … your dog simply won't understand. That is unless your energy is reflected in your tone of voice (see VOICE COMMANDS) but even then it's not the words your dog is relating to but rather your **energy** and **intention**.

To **reassure a scared dog the process is different to that of reassuring a scared child**. To reassure a scared child they need soft words and perhaps a hug.

To similarly **reassure and stroke an unbalanced dog is to positively reinforce the fearful or anxious behaviour**. The best way you can reassure your dog is through your own confident body language and close proximity, but to only stroke them the split second they themselves are calm.

The idea of positively rewarding calm behaviour with touch is achieved by quietly stroking your dog when they are relaxed. Stop the stroking if they leave their neutral state, recommence when your dog is calm again ... this is called **The Nothing Exercise.**

The Nothing Exercise along with all other videos to accompany this book can be found on Dailymotion (a video-sharing site similar to YouTube). Search for Yorkshire Dog Whisperer and select CHANNELS (NOT Videos or Playlists). This ensures you get access to all the videos in one place. I won't print any other video title pages, but will take it as given you know they are available.

NEUTRAL BODY LANGUAGE TO REWARD WITH STROKING

- Ears relaxed, not pricked up in excitement
- Fairly still or gently fluid moving tail and body, not a fast wagging tail (over excited), an upright alert tail or a fearful tucked under tail
- Relaxed, not tense/stiff stance or shaking body
- Relaxed breathing and mouth, not anxious panting or licking
- Standing up, sitting or lying down with all four paws on the floor, not one paw held up off the floor
- Calm eyes, not a hard stare or a nervous non-direct look

YOUR BODY LANGUAGE

Most of us don't realise we are doing it when we take a step backwards, or lean away from our dogs. If you do this your dog reads your **body language** to be that of a less confident dog below them in the family hierarchy. By giving ground or territory you are in your dogs eyes forfeiting your leadership role.

The correct body language can help in getting your dog to take you seriously, and take more note of what you are asking them to do. If you establish yourself as being above your dog in the family hierarchy … then your dog should never disrespect you by growling at you.

*C*ASE STUDY

I visited a client who had a 4 month old small mixed breed puppy. The puppy was growling at the owner when she tried to remove the puppy from the pup's comfy basket.

The lady had previously had a bad experience with a dog, and was displaying hesitant body language. She withdrew her hand, and didn't hold her ground. The puppy took this lack of confidence (leaders are always confident) as a sign her owner was below her in the family hierarchy ... and felt justified in growling her disagreement at being removed from the bed.

As soon as I showed my client how not to hesitate, or pull away from the puppy ... the puppy stopped growling and quite happily came off her bed. In this case the owner was more confident taking hold of the puppy's collar.

TIP – Always ensure your dog wears a collar round the house, it just makes handling easier.

Until you get a handle on the fact - that dogs communicate with **energy, read your body language and** and have a **hierarchy** - any unwanted behaviour may never go away. This won't be your dog's fault, since to dogs human languages and ways of communicating really are a foreign language.

COMMUNICATION EXERCISE

NOTE - This exercise should only be done with dogs who don't display food guarding behaviour.

I have developed this simple exercise for my clients to teach them:

1. To communicate a message using your energy, a noise and positive reinforcement (the treat).

2. To hold your ground as a dog at the top of the family hierarchy would.

COMMUNICATION EXERCISE

- Crouch down and **hold a dog treat in your hand**, protruding forwards so that your dog can easily take it.
- You then need to hold your space and **not retract your hand**. Instead use your other hand to move your dog away (pushing them on their chest) whilst simultaneously making a distinct noise. Your energy intensity is reflected in the level of your noise, and should reflect your dog's energy level.
- The instant your dog stops trying to eat the treat and moves away from your space ... **give your dog the treat**.

2. COMMUNICATION TOOLS

The main communication tools we have are:

1. **VARYING ENERGY LEVELS AND EMOTIONS**
2. **OUR PHYSICAL BODY LANGUAGE**
3. **FOOD REWARDS**
4. **SHORT TERM CONSEQUENCES**

1. VARYING ENERGY LEVELS

To demonstrate to your dog there is nothing to be reactive over your best tool is your confidence.

Dogs have learned behaviour patterns, but they also live in the moment. The key to changing a dog's behaviour is for you to join them in inhabiting the present, and to emotionally let go of any past bad experiences which then allows you to **project the required confidence to help rehabilitate your reactive dog.**

You can also use **excited energy** to act as a **reward**, for instance after a recall or the split second a scared dog makes that first step towards something they are unsure of.

An example of this is with a dog who won't walk upstairs. By getting really excited it helps to over come their initial fear (fear and excitement are closely linked), and then when they make that first step use **split second timing** in rewarding the action with excited stroking. **You have about 2 seconds to either agree or disagree with behaviour.** In this way you are communicating your wish for them to climb the stairs.

You can also use your energy to **disagree** with an action. For instance if your dog is nuisance barking or about to steal some food you need to project your disagreement using a noise or command word at the appropriate energy intensity.

If your dog's energy intensity is greater than yours they will simply ignore you.

Your energy needs to **equal** that of your dog's in order for them to listen to you. It should never be greater than your dog's which would induce fear.

To show your disagreement with your dog I believe following the mother dogs example works well - i.e. remaining calm and issuing a gentle nudge and/or a sound of disagreement.

When you nudge or gently push your dog away, you can combine it with a sound of disagreement. This needs to be a distinct sound or word, or even a growl and will vary to the individual.

I often use a "shhh" noise like Cesar Millan - "The Dog Whisperer" of US TV fame (my initial inspiration - but working for myself I have been able to develop my own less dominance based techniques). It's worth experimenting to find out what noise your dog listens to the best. You can't be embarrassed ... even if your dog listens to you best when you growl at them!

A nudge can either be with your hand, leg or a gentle pull on the collar ... but should never be with your foot so as not to be confused with a kick. The nudge will obviously vary in firmness depending on the size of the dog, bigger dogs needing a firmer nudge, but **it should never be hard or cause any pain. You are not punishing your dog, rather disagreeing with them.**

Once your dog understands your noise means you disagree with them, you can **use your noise without the physical touch** (a push on the chest - as in the COMMUNICATION EXERCISE) to indicate you wish your dog to cease doing something ... it can be very usefully to stop your dog doing something naughty from a distance!

2. YOUR PHYSICAL BODY LANGUAGE

I believe that the traditional dominance theory is flawed when dog trainers dominate dogs to such an extent that results in a dog shaking (a sign of trauma - for example a dog will shake after being involved in a fight), before submitting or relaxing.

In general I believe that there are **no right or wrong training methods ... as long as no pain, fear or trauma are involved**. Each dog and handler combination are unique and as such need to find what works best for them.

As noted I believe the traumatic aspect of the dominance theory is not one that should be employed. However, I think it is important that we have an understanding of the dominance theory in as far as what message our body language is transmitting to our dogs. You obviously don't want to totally dominant your dog, but in order for your dog to listen to you and take you seriously knowing the correct body language can be very useful.

Moving away/giving ground = Further down the pecking order

Moving forwards/holding space = Higher up the hierarchy

Body language is also important when working with a nervous dog. It's best to let a nervous dog approach you, and to **project less energy** you can **turn away** from the dog and **crouch down**.

More energy is emitted from your front with your face, and especially your eyes focusing your intent. **That's why when meeting a new dog it's best to avoid looking at them, and allowing them to come to you.** If they don't want to engage then it's best to respect this and continue to ignore them.

3. FOOD REWARDS

Food rewards are great and often can be combined with other communication tools. They can be used for the training of basic commands, and to communicate **rewards** such as when your dog moves away from your food ... the result is they get a treat.

Treats can also be used to make a **new association** with something that previously your dog didn't enjoy. Food, combined with the right energy and body language can help a dog overcome a bad experience.

High value food rewards are great for **recall training** and should be offered on a regular basis as a good training exercise … recall training should be lifelong.

Not all dogs are food orientated and as such quiet or excited stroking (depending on the circumstances) can be substituted for a food reward, as well as correctly timed verbal praise.

4. SHORT TERM CONSEQUENCES

Consequences can also involve food and energy with positive associations. In other cases you might employ a negative consequence. For example, by removing your dog from the room for a short period if they are jumping all over any non-dog loving visitors. By allowing them back into the room when they are calm, and consistently removing them for short periods every time they jump … you are using a consequence to communicate the message not to jump.

3. NATURE AND NURTURE

Before we move on to PART TWO and look at specific behavioural problems, it should be noted that I believe a dog is born with a certain personality trait (NATURE). But as to how this dog turns out will depend on a combination of its base personality, breed characteristics, energy levels and the influence of the owner (NURTURE).

If you observe a litter of puppies there are always different characters - some displaying more confidence than others.

THREE MAIN PERSONALITY TYPES

- **NERVOUS** - alarm barkers
- **COMMUNICATORS** - friendly and natural followers
- **CONFIDENT** - born leaders

Dogs who are natural COMMUNICATORS are the easiest to train, naturally NERVOUS dogs can bond closely to their chosen human, but need the right instructions to thrive, and more CONFIDENT dogs need more confident leaders if they are ever to follow directions.

Paul White is an ecologist who has studied man-made packs of dogs who help to guard flocks of sheep in Romania. He recognises these **different characters**, along with the fact that dogs have a **hierarchy**.

"Dogs like humans have different characters, some are bolder, some bark louder and there are leaders and some who prefer to follow. There tends to be a hierarchy within the pack which is made up of individuals of different ages, size and experience. These dogs are tough and aggressive but alone they are no match for a wolf or a bear. Their strength is in their numbers, pack cohesion and dynamics, and it takes a good shepherd to put an effective team together".

TIP - The easiest way to attempt to pick a natural COMMUNICATOR - is to identify the quietest and the most confident characters ... and then choose your puppy from the remaining litter mates.

PART TWO

PREVENTION AND CURE FOR BEHAVIOURAL PROBLEMS

1. PULLING ON THE LEAD

PREVENTION

For puppies I would always recommend trying a back fastening harness first to prevent them chewing on the lead. As they get older they can then progress onto a front fastening harness which can help reduce pulling.

Smaller dogs in particular are better on a front fastening harness, while larger dogs might walk better with a simple slip lead at the very top of their neck (thus avoiding crushing the wind pipe).

As well as selecting the right lead you also need to put the time in to communicate with your dog you want them to walk on a loose lead, focused on you (instructions to achieve this in CURE section).

DIFFERENT TYPES OF LEADS

FRONT FASTENING HARNESSES

A great option for smaller dogs with delicate necks, or for any size of who dog who responds well to a harness. Back fastening harnesses are designed for pulling and are best for puppies and working sled dogs.

NOTE - The front clip needs to be at the top of your dog's chest, not in the middle, to prevent your dog's front legs being impeded whilst walking.

SLIP LEADS

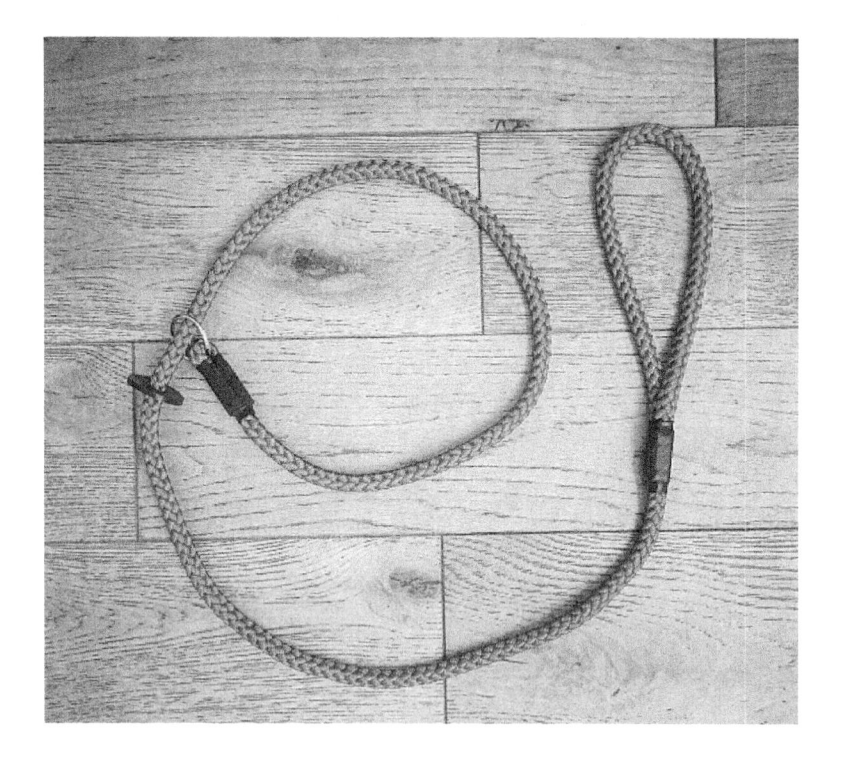

Good for medium or larger dogs (and smaller very reactive dogs). Placed higher rather than lower down your dog's neck – having the lead in this position (above the collar, just behind the ears) gives you more control and doesn't put too much pressure on your dog's windpipe.

If you do need to use a slip lead on a smaller reactive dog make sure it is a wide, preferably flat lead so as not to put too much pressure on their necks.

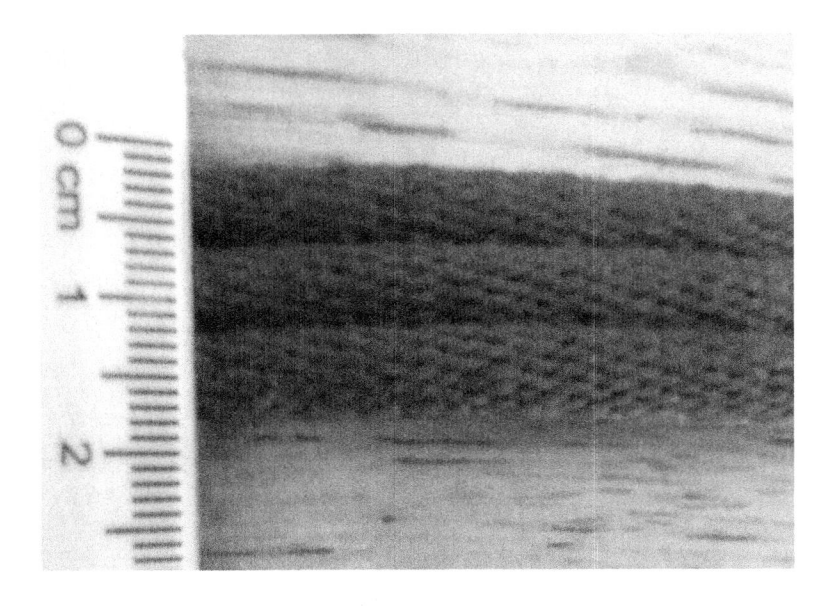

Flat airweb style slip leads are better for reactive smaller dogs.

FIGURE OF EIGHT SLIP LEADS OR HALTIES

This type of lead should be a last resort, and might not be necessary if you follow the instructions coming shortly which explain how to get your dog to walk on a loose lead.

However, for some owners these might be the answer so I have also included guidelines for fitting a halti style lead.

MUZZLE HEADCOLLARS

A headcollar with a muzzle component. Good for dogs who are reactive ... it might be worth sewing the muzzle together in a position which allows your dog to pant, but not to bite.

NOTE - These muzzles are not as effective as traditional muzzles - they still allow nipping, but not full on biting. However, they don't look as intimidating as traditional muzzles.

CURE

You are struggling to walk your dog without excessive pulling on the lead, and have missed out the basic training. I am going to walk you threw how to get even the most severe pullers walking with you on a loose lead. I am also going to explain how to then easily get your dog to walk at heel off the lead.

THE STOP/START METHOD OF WALKING ON A LOOSE LEAD

1. Fit your dog with either a front fastening harness (smaller dogs), or a slip lead. Your lead should be approximately 1 meter in length.
2. Hold the top of the lead in one hand, the lead needs to be able to fall loose and should not be grasped further down away from the handle.

3. Take one step forwards, and then deliberately stop, stamping your f___ You can also stop and then take 2 step backwards. As your dog moves forwards ahead of you, pull them back as the end of the lead is reached and the lead goes tight. You need to give a firm tug (equaling the energy and size of your dog) and say any disagreeing word or sound in a firm voice.
4. Repeat step 3, and keep repeating step 3 until your dog halts with you without the lead going tight. This means no tug is needed, and instead instantaneous praise (within 2 seconds) in an excited voice is given.
5. Now add in treats when your dog looks at your face. Treats only need be used initially to reinforce that you are asking your dog to walk and focus on you.
6. You can add some changes of direction into the mix and lots of praise when your dog follows you on a loose lead. You need to engage your dog in a high excited voice.

If you imagine yourself as the centre point in a circle, with the lead being able to plot a circle around you if pulled taut. Anytime the lead goes tight i.e. reaches the edge of the circumference of your circle you need to express your disagreement that your dog isn't walking with you.

Your tug on the lead needs to be not too weak, and not to strong. It needs to **equal your dogs energy in order for them to listen to you**, and by it's self isn't as effective. Your tug needs to be combined with your projected energy and intention, reflected in your voice control ("Shhh" or "Hey").

This voice control word needs to reflect your indignation that your dog isn't walking with you. Only then when you have mastered achieving a loose lead should you think about introducing the command "heel" (see LOOSE HEEL OFF THE LEAD).

Asking your dog to walk with you is the first half of the message, the second half is as soon as your dog looks up or stops with you without the lead going tight. This is when they need to be rewarded with enthusiastic verbal praise. Basically you are communicating the message "no thank you" to a tight lead and "yes please" to a loose one.

Turn it into a habit to not leave your house (keep stopping) until the lead is loose and your dog has made eye contact. Be patient and remember that the last behaviour you end up with (tight or loose lead) is the behaviour your dog believes you are asking for. You might also want to reset your dog before walking past other dogs or through a busy area.

LOOSE HEEL OFF THE LEAD

If you have mastered walking your dog on a loose lead, you are only one small step away from being able to ask your dog to walk at heel off lead. I am not talking about an obedience level heel whereby your dog is close to your leg and continually maintaining eye contact, but more of a loose heel which can be handy on a walk.

LOOSE HEEL

1. Attach a long 2-3 meter lead to your dog's harness (harnesses need to be used with long leads to prevent neck insures).
2. Initially shorten the lead to 1 meter in length. Do as in the previous exercise to achieve a loose lead.
3. Once a loose lead is achieved, practise dropping the long lead whilst continuing to walk forwards. If your dog goes to break away from you quickly stand on the lead and verbally cue your dog with the "heel" command (the instant you step on the lead). Your command needs to be in a low firm voice, and you have to have the right intention i.e. you need to be thinking the right thoughts, basically that your dog is going to stay with you no matter what! Eventually you will be able to do this without the aid of a long lead.
4. Practise this exercise at home for a few weeks with no distractions around, before progressing to low level distractions on your walk.

USING HALTI STYLE LEADS

Hopefully you won't need to use a halti. However, if for some reason you do due to health issues, or you have a very high energy, large dog or even a smaller scent dog whose main focus is on sniffing (and not on you) then the following might be helpful.

Initially use **treats** to distract and then reward your dog the split second the figure of eight is fitted to give a to good association with the new lead.

If your dog does ever display any discomfort and attempts to paw the halti off – you need to disagree with this behaviour with your chosen noise, and then use an enthusiastic voice to encourage your dog to move forwards.

If your dog still doesn't listen include a touch with your noise, or take hold of your dog's collar and lift upwards (this is also necessary if your dog tries to rub their face along the floor). Running with your dog can help to distract them.

You need to be very patient and end on the right behaviour. Only take the halti off when your dog is not pawing at it. Little and often is best to start with.

It can be a good idea to double lead your dog initially ... this has two benefits:

- Using a second lead attached to your dogs collar or harness can **reduce the pressure/discomfort** your dog feels from using a halti style lead. Make sure you are only pulling on the second lead, not on the halti.
- If your dog does manage to get out of the new lead you have a back up one attached.

TIP - Never pull on a halti style lead as this will only tighten them, and cause more discomfort.

NOTE - To get your dog accustomed to wearing a muzzle you can use the same technique as described here for the halti.

2. DOGS WHO WON'T WALK ON THE LEAD/USE STAIRS/JUMP INTO THE CAR

I have categorised these behavioural problems together, because the CURE is basically the same. **This method is also great for introducing puppies to walking on the lead.**

PREVENTION

If you always carry your puppy up and downstairs/into the car ... and continue to do so for too long, they might think this is the way it should be done. As soon as your puppy is big enough encourage them to do it by themselves.

To overcome these hurdles you need to turn into the most enthusiastic **cheerleader**! You also need a **front fastening harness**, so that you can pull your dog knowing you aren't going to hurt them.

For walking on the lead you can start training around the home from a young age. Be very encouraging, use excited energy the first few times your puppy is on the lead. Little and often is best to start with. The first training session may only be a couple of minutes.

Treats can also be used to positively reinforce the experience, and as goals to strive towards if any reluctance to move forward is experienced.

Disagree with any **lead chewing** by giving a quick flick of the lead and make your disagreeing noise whilst leaning forwards. Using a back fastening harness initially (and a tighter lead) should help prevent lead chewing.

CURE

Some dogs take longer to get the message about walking on a lead, going up and down stairs/getting into the car ... or you have unintentionally communicated the wrong message.

The technique is simple. Attach a lead to the harness and pull from the front with a constant pressure. Simultaneously use an excited voice to encourage your dog to move.

As soon as they take even just one step forwards/move onto the first step/or jump into the car ... you need to vamp up the excitement even more and reward with lots of excited petting and more verbal praise. "Good boy!" "Well done!" Your timing through excited praise and stroking is communicating the message ... moving forwards is good.

The main emotions you can't feel in this exercise are EMBARRASSMENT or PITY ... just go for it!!

NOTE - Some dogs may initially need you to use an additional lead as well as the front fastening harness (a normal slip lead or collar and lead). Two leads will only need to be used for a short period.

3. DOG REACTIVE DOGS

There can be many reasons for your dog to become reactive towards other dogs. Therefore different approaches are needed to help cure this problem.

PREVENTION

To prevent your dog from becoming dog reactive you need to socialise them regularly from an early age. Puppies learn social skills, they aren't born with them. Even dogs who are natural COMMUNICATORS with a friendly disposition still need to be socialised.

I wouldn't advise letting puppies off the lead until they are old enough, and experienced enough to be confident around other dogs. Other larger dogs with a high prey drive might also mistake your puppy as a small furry animal to chase.

CASE STUDY

Before realising the importance of how critical the time is when puppies learn lasting life lessons, I made the mistake of having one of my own dogs off the lead too soon. She was a jack russell puppy and very tiny, we were in the middle of an empty playing field ... when an escaped Labrador came and scooped her up and ran away with her. The Lab did drop her after about 30 seconds, but the damage both mentally and physically had been done.

A lack of knowledge on my behalf meant that I didn't straight away socialise her with as many dogs as possible. As it turned out I ended up isolating her from other dogs. I was EMBARRASSED, and I became very ANXIOUS every time I spotted another dog.

It wasn't until years later that we both managed to find some peace around other dogs, after I realised my emotions (ANXIETY and EMBARRASSMENT) contributed to Amber's on going fear. I hope to spread the knowledge that I have acquired to help prevent other dogs and owners suffering as Amber and I did.

So, the other main prevention apart from socialisation, is if you do get in a bad situation always remain CALM. It won't help your dog if you express ANGER towards the other owner.

CURE

You have a dog reactive dog and you no longer enjoy your walks, and if possible will avoid all other dogs ... sound familiar?!

However, there is some hope. There are ways that you can greatly improve your dog's behaviour, and you might actually start enjoying your walks again. You may still cross the road to create a buffer of space for your dog, but you will do so in a confident manner without your dog reacting.

Depending on why your dog is barking/reacting to other dogs you might need to change your tactics. Dogs who make the most noise might be NERVOUS AGGRESSIVE; dogs who are silent with a hard stare could have the worst intentions; where as other silent dogs can simply be NERVOUS.

There are two main areas I am going to cover - walking your dog calmly **on the lead**, and once you have mastered this **rehabilitation** - which looks towards having your dog interacting with other dogs **off the lead**.

ON THE LEAD

Methods vary for different dogs:

1. OVER EXCITED DOGS
2. CONFIDENT AGGRESSIVE DOGS
3. NERVOUS NON-AGGRESSIVE DOGS
4. NERVOUS AGGRESSIVE DOGS

1. OVER EXCITED DOGS

Some dogs aren't aggressive in their intentions, but can whine and bark in excitement when they see other dogs. The barking can sometimes be mistaken for aggression, but these dogs are barking because they are on the lead and being stopped from going over to play with other dogs.

In this instance you need to do **two things** - teach your dog to **walk on a loose lead focused on you** (and not on the other dogs); communicate the **message that they will only be allowed to go near the other dogs once they themselves are calm.**

Follow the instructions in the PULLING ON THE LEAD chapter to achieve a loose lead. You need to practise this at first in a place with no distractions.

The best method to communicate the new message is by providing a **consequence**. There are two ways you can do this.

- Come in between the other dogs and your dog and ask for a **sit** using the collar, and then release/move towards the other dogs when your dog is calm.
- The second your dog starts to bark **turn around and walk away**, the instance they stop **turn back around** and give your dog a loose lead to walk back towards the other dog. Repeat.

It's worth using both methods depending on the circumstances, but in particular **initially** I would **focus on the walking away method in a large open space**. As always you need to be **100% consistent** to communicate the new message to your dog. It is a good idea to drain your dogs energy on a long walk, before completing this exercise. You don't want to set your dog up to fail.

TIP - For medium or large over excited dogs you might consider using a doggy backpack to drain their energy.

You fill the backpack with bags of rice which weigh 10% of your dog's total body weight. By using a backpack it's like you have walked your dog twice as far. Only suitable for healthy adult dogs.

2. CONFIDENT AGGRESSIVE DOGS

A review from one of my clients with a large, CONFIDENT dog in the "hard stare" camp. We saw a big improvement on the lead after one session:

"Wow what can I say! I have a very reactive Sharpei that has seen several different dog trainers and he's never liked being in the company of other dogs! After only 1 hour session today my Sharpei was walking by the side of other dogs and in a field surrounded by dogs! We were in control and Kaiser was relatively calm. This is the first time in his 2 and a half yrs that he's ever done this. I'm so elated and can't wait to see his progress.

These owners had tried various methods including food rewards to have positive associations with new dogs ... but their dog was only interested in challenging all other dogs. Food as a distraction can only be used once you are able to control your dog and keep them relatively calm - see STEP 4.

You need a large open space with other dog walkers near to try the following exercise.

STEP 1 – WALKING AT HEEL

Start by getting the right lead and practising **walking at heel on a loose lead** (see PULLING ON THE LEAD). For non-reactive dogs it's fine to let them walk in front of you if they aren't pulling on the lead. For dog reactive dogs it's very important to have your dog's front shoulder in line with your leg, or even positioned behind you.

As the saying goes "the devil is in the detail"... it might appear to be nonsensical to always walk your dog at heel (or in some cases even behind you), but for a dog reactive dog it is important for you to be in the lead so that it's your energy that meets the other dog first.

If you let your dog walk in front of you they will set the tone for the meeting *not* you.

STEP 2 – WALKING IN NEUTRAL

You need to be relaxed, yet walk with confidence and not react physically or mentally to situations. Ignoring distractions or other dog walkers is imperative. Your energy should be focused on your dog alone, and asking them to walk with you on a loose lead.

Once you have achieved loose lead walking **look where you are going**, instead of constantly lowering your gaze to your dog and you will project a more confident energy.

You need to remain in neutral so that your body doesn't unconsciously give your dog messages to react. If you stay in a neutral, unemotional state your dog has more chance to also remain in neutral.

By giving **eye contact** to other dog owners you are removing yourself from neutral, and directing your dog's attention towards the object that draws your gaze. This is the exact opposite of what you need to do with a dog reactive dog. If you know someone walking another dog, and need to say hello then do so at the last minute without prolonged eye contact.

You need to **mentally relax** your shoulders so tension isn't transmitted down your lead arm. Slow abdominal breathing may help you to relax or thinking about something else may distract your brain. Alternatively, talking to a friend as a distraction is a good way to get past another dog, or focusing on your dog - see STEP 4.

If there is any reaction you need to disagree with the behaviour, and reward a calm reaction (as described in the next section) or anytime your dog looks at you.

COMMUNICATE YOU WANT CA\ BEHAVIOUR

If your dog reacts with a hard stare and/or high intensity barking you need to employ the snow plough manoeuvre.

The idea is that you catch the reaction before it erupts into full blown out of control lunging or barking, and redirect your dogs attention back onto you. **Only if your dog is out of control and can't be redirected should the snow plough technique be employed** i.e. it is only appropriate to use when your dog's intensity is very high.

NOTE - These steps are a training exercise to be done in a large open area. Whilst out on a normal walk it might be best not to employ the snow plough, but rather to keep moving forwards in a confident manner and provide a bubble of space around your dog. You need to walk as though you always meant to walk around the oncoming dog, with confidence and purpose. Your dog is at heel, and you continue to stay in neutral and ignore all other dogs

THE SNOW PLOUGH

- You need to **turn your back** to the other dog, and then **drive your dog away** from them. By turning your back to the new dog you are demonstrating there is nothing to be afraid of. By moving your dog away and claiming ground you are claiming territory. As you walk towards your dog you might need to push your dog out of the way gently with your knees if they fail to move (this is only necessary with large very out of control dogs).
- Ask for a **"sit"** to distract your dog. You might need to click your fingers (or give a gentle tug on the lead/collar) to gain your dog's attention before asking for the sit.
- Once you have achieved a sit, and the split second your dog is relaxed and not focused on the other dog, you can **stroke** your dog with no verbal praise (the sound of your voice might get your dog excited again) and/or give them a **treat**. This acts as positive reinforcement. The timing of the reward is critical ... your dog needs to understand what they have done right.

An alternative to the snow plough can be just to hold your dog's collar, ask for a sit (give a gentle tug if they ignore you) and then silently stroke them as a reward when they are quiet/relaxed.

If you give affection, be it verbal or through touch, and your dog *isn't* calm you are simply positively reinforcing unwanted behaviour through this mis-timed affection.

If your dog starts to react in a smaller way you can also try giving a tug on the lead (as learned in achieving loose lead walking), or a slight nudge with your leg (not your foot which could be misinterpreted as a kick) combined with a your chosen deep, growly voice command or disagreeing noise.

Basically you are asking your dog to focus on you, and not the other dogs. The split second they do reward them with enthusiastic vocal praise, exactly the same principals apply as with loose lead walking. If your dog looks at you they need to be rewarded instantly.

STEP 3 - GETTING CLOSER

After mastering the neutral, loose lead, heel work you can then progress to walking slowly closer to other dogs. Your dog needs space to gradually acclimatise to being relaxed around other dogs.

You need them **totally focused on you**, this means not allowing them to even sniff the ground when walking through an area with other dogs in.

It might be easier to start with other dogs who are on the lead, projecting less energy than dogs racing round off the lead. You can slowly progress to being near dogs off the lead.

Another possibility is to ask a friend with a non-reactive dog to help. Give them instructions on how to behave - you need to start off about 20 meters apart, ignore each other and keep walking past each other getting gradually closer.

You should end up walking calmly together but without allowing your dogs to sniff each other on the short leads. Then get your friend to walk just ahead of you when passing other dogs.

TIP - Don't let a reactive dog sniff other dogs when on a short lead, they feel trapped and their reaction can be unpredictable.

Also bear in mind that if another off lead dog approaches you, it is best to ignore this dog (including no eye contact) and if necessary turn around and confidently walk away in the opposite direction.

Be patient, confident and relaxed yet assertive. Remember the best way you can help your dog is if you don't PITY them, get EMBARRASSED, FRUSTRATED or ANGRY. Just staying calm and unemotional is the best way you can help an unbalanced, reactive dog.

STEP 4 - DISTRACTION

Some dogs and owners might do well just using steps 1-3, where as others will benefit from adding a distraction and asking for even more of their dogs focus.

This can have a two fold benefit, distracting more of your dog's attention away from the other dog, and also a good way for owners who find it hard to remain confident to achieve a neutral state of mind. You have to concentrate on getting your dog's attention, not on panicking about their reaction.

DISTRACTING YOUR DOG

- Call our dog's name in a high excited voice to get their attention onto you.
- Use high value treats (or a toy for non-food orientated dogs) to help gain their attention. A few very small treats can be given from your non-lead hand.
- Repeat this exercise when no other dogs are around, as well as when passing other dogs.

NOTE - Dogs who are out of control/very stressed won't eat, therefore it's important to to complete steps 1-3 before attempting distraction techniques.

3. NERVOUS NON-AGGRESSIVE DOGS

A dog who is fearful of other dogs and doesn't excessively bark, but rather tucks their tail between their legs and tries to run away will respond best if you remain calm and confident when you approach other friendly dogs. You need to communicate through your own body language that there is nothing to fear.

If you remain in confident neutral, your dog will feel reassured and be more likely to relax and follow your lead.

Fearful dogs need reassurance from a calm leader. They are different from children in that if you touch and reassure them with soft words they will take this as positive reinforcement of the fearful behaviour. This is why you only stroke your dog when they are calm/in a balanced neutral state (see GENERAL ANXIETY & FIREWORKS).

Follow STEPS 1 - 4 in CONFIDENT DOGS/OVER EXCITED DOGS but with no need for any disagreement (no snow plough) as your dog isn't aggressively barking/lunging or demonstrating a hard stare, but rather is quiet and fearful.

You might need to run and use an excited voice if your dog is hesitant to walk on the lead (see DOGS WHO WON'T WALK ON THE LEAD), or simply remain quiet and confident with your dog walking at heel.

You need to learn which method works best for you and your own individual handler/dog combination. You should continue walking up and down, slowly getting closer until you are walking next to the other dog (or behind) still ignoring them ... with no reaction.

Make sure the owner of the other dog is confident that their dog is friendly, **ignore both dogs**. If relaxed sniffing behaviour ensures ... great let them say hello. Alternatively maybe ask if you can walk with them for a minute, or just walk confidently by. Try and end with a positive, confident interaction.

TIP - For particularly nervous dogs as an initial introduction - walk them behind other dogs on the lead. The back view of another dog has less energy, and is less intimidating than approaching from the front.

CASE STUDY

I had one client who had an incredibly NERVOUS cockapoo. His initial safe distance off the lead away from his owner was only about 2 metres.

At the start of the session his owner confided in me that her husband claimed their dog was better on walks (moved further away and interacted with other dogs without barking) when she didn't accompany them, but that secretly she didn't believe him.

By the end of the session her cockapoo had graduated to a safe distance of about 10-20 metres and was interacting with other dogs off the lead, and no longer barking at them.

The only difference between the start and the end of the session was that I asked her to ignore all the other dogs in the park (she initially ignored my advice and stroked my cockapoo Cesar in greeting ... the instantaneous reaction from her own dog was to bark) and remain in confident neutral.

She conceded by the end of the session that her husband might have been telling her the truth after all!

4. NERVOUS AGGRESSIVE DOGS

Follow STEPS 1-4 as with CONFIDENT DOGS/OVER EXCITED DOGS. To disagree use the snow plough or the holding the collar alternative. Each dog is different, if these techniques don't work you may need to use a similar technique as to when introducing a puppy to other dogs.

As when socialising puppies you need to make NERVOUS dogs feel secure. If your **small nervous aggressive dog** reaches high intensity barking the following can be helpful.

NERVOUS AGGRESSIVE TECHNIQUE FOR SMALL DOGS

- Crouch down and bring your dog close to you (between your knees) to give them somewhere they can shelter and feel safe.
- Give a gentle tug on their collar, possibly use your disagreeing noise, and ask for a "sit".
- Quietly stroke them once they are calm.

NOTE - This is designed as a training exercise in a large open space when the other dog isn't too near. Whilst out on a normal walk it might be best *not* to employ this method, but rather to keep moving forwards in a confident manner and provide a bubble of space around your dog. You need to walk as though you always meant to walk around the oncoming dog, with confidence and purpose. Your dog is at heel, and you continue to stay in neutral and ignore all other dogs.

CONCLUSION FOR WALKING ON THE LEAD

In practice it can take time and patience to achieve improved confidence for you and your dog. Everything might not go according to plan every time, especially in the beginning.

Don't become downhearted after a bad experience, rather try experimenting. Think about was my dog's shoulder right next to my leg, or can I try walking my dog behind me when passing other dogs? Do I need to avoid walking in enclosed spaces? Will I have more success walking behind other dogs on the lead, before walking abreast with them? Is my dog better with or without distractions? Was my dog walking with me on a loose lead?

Most importantly don't give up, all dogs can be improved and many even cured.

TIP - If you have no choice but to enter a narrow passing area, make sure your dog is either behind you, or on the opposite side to any approaching dogs. If possible turn around and wait for the other dog to exit before you enter with your dog.

TIP - Walk with your dog on the opposite side when passing any oncoming dogs. Always swap sides behind your back so your dog is never in front of you.

TIP - If you want to talk to a fellow dog walker, but are worried your dog will be reactive - position your dog behind you and don't interact with your dog or the other person's dog.

REHABILITATION

You have mastered walking your dog calmly on the lead, and now want to progress to letting your dog socialise off the lead.

Some NERVOUS NON-AGGRESSIVE dogs can make this leap effortlessly, as long as you remain calm and confident and ignore other new dogs. Others may need their confidence building up as you would when socialising a puppy.

SOCIALISATION TIPS

- **Start socialisation with other dogs who are on the lead, before progressing to more high energy dogs off the lead.**
- **Crouching down can create a safe place for your dog to come and hide.**
- **Always check if the other dog is friendly, if the owner isn't confident in their answer don't feel bad about walking away.**

Any dog who shows aggression towards other dogs may need slower rehabilitation in working towards off lead social interactions. You basically need to communicate a new set of instructions on how to behave around other dogs, in a safe way.

Even more CONFIDENT dogs can be rehabilitated to be calm around other calm dogs ... but it should be remembered that if challenged it will be their instinct to reply in kind.

NOTE - Not all dogs are suitable candidates to be rehabilitated and let off the lead in public spaces.

You may not be able to let your reactive dog sniff other dogs on a short lead (I would suggest the **"no sniffing rule"** be applied on a **short lead**) as their reaction can be unpredictable. Dogs feel trapped on a short lead. However, the use of a long training lead will allow your dog the freedom to socialise and sniff without feeling trapped, but still allow you to control the situation.

You need to have **control of your dogs head direction**, hence the head collar. The idea is to let your dog interact more freely with other **off lead dogs**, but at the first sign of aggression to make your disagreeing noise and turn your dogs head away.

In order to start the rehabilitation process you will need a 2-3 meter training lead and a headcollar muzzle (see **PULLING ON THE LEAD - USING HALTI STYLE LEADS** for how to get your dog used to wearing a headcollar muzzle).

This directional control and disagreement will allow you to give your dog a new set of instructions i.e. to be calm around other dogs.

TIP - Don't stand in one place but rather keep walking forwards ... forward momentum can help distract your dog.

Once you have had lots of success using this method, you can then think about removing the training lead, but keeping the muzzle on until you TRUST your dog. It might be advisable to always have some form of muzzle on a CONFIDENT dog who may now not initiate a confrontation, but may still respond if another dog does.

It's best to keep your dog away from dogs on the lead, and focus on other off lead dogs. You may want to consider **day care** so your dog can meet off lead dogs in a controlled setting.

Any good day care will assess your dog and introduce them to their pack in a safe way. The staff at the day care won't be emotionally involved, and will have no bad experiences to reference which might drain their confidence.

A good rule of thumb is to be honest about your dog's behaviour, and to only try the day care centres where the staff respond with confidence (the same holds true when asking other dog owners if their dog is friendly - only socialise your dog with other dogs when their owners give a confident response).

4. TRAFFIC REACTIVE DOGS

PREVENTION

Walk your new dog next to busy roads on a short loose lead at heel (see PULLING ON THE LEAD)... and ignore the traffic. You need to remain in your calm state to communicate to your dog there is nothing to be afraid of.

CURE

The cure for dogs who are scared or lunge at traffic is actually very similar to that of DOG REACTIVE DOGS. The main difference is that it can be implemented quicker as traffic is inanimate rather than other dogs who project energy for your dog to feed off.

You need to practise walking your dog on a **short loose lead**, with their front shoulder next to your leg and without excessive pulling before going near a road (see PULLING ON THE LEAD).

Once you have mastered this try walking next to a road with a large verge. Start at the edge of the verge furthest away from the traffic and walk purposefully, whilst directing none of your energy towards the vehicles and with your dog on your side furthest from the traffic.

Dogs are so in tuned with us they even pick up where you are directing your eyes. Avoid any **eye contact** with the traffic, stay in your **neutral** so that your dog has a chance to remain in theirs.

If your dog starts to lunge and bark at the traffic intensely, employ the snow plough manoeuvre or the alternative to the snow plough for smaller dogs. In this instance turn your back to the traffic. Repeat this exercise and slowly get closer to the road. If your energy and intention are correct, then it shouldn't take long for your dog to stop being scared or lunging at traffic.

TIP - Walk your dog on your side away from the traffic.

5. PEOPLE REACTIVE DOGS

PREVENTION

As well as your dog needing to learn how to socialise with other dogs, they also need to learn how to interact with people. No dog is born fully socialised.

Remember for dogs who live in a hierarchical society it is natural for them to growl at lower ranking members. Higher ranking positions are characterised by confidence and holding your space/claiming your territory. If you can master the COMMUNICATION EXERCISE then you have taken the first step in becoming your dog's calm leader.

In order to give your dog the best chance of becoming well socialised they need to be regularly exposed and handled by lots of people from an early age.

Dogs start learning life lessons from only a few weeks old. That's why it's important to buy a puppy from a breeder who understands this, and provides appropriate living conditions and socialisation.

It's worth taking your new puppy out regularly to busy places and letting as many people interact with them as possible. As long as they don't go on the floor it's a great idea to start socialising them in public places from 8 weeks old - ideally after their first vaccinations have been administered.

You also need to fulfill your calm leadership role. If your dog shows any aggression or barks at another person when they are in your vicinity you need to disagree, and possibly provide a consequence.

For instance, if you were sitting on the sofa with your dog, and they growled at another person your instantaneous reaction should be disagreement. You should make your disagreeing noise, and calmly just push them off the sofa (or for smaller puppies lift them down safely) ... thus also providing a consequence by removing them from the situation.

An alternative consequence for a barking dog might be to place your dog on the lead until they are calm ... remember leads can be very useful inside the house as direct calming tools ... or to remove them from the room until they are calm.

CURE

To cure your dog from being people reactive is to know your dog's temperament, and to train the people who come into contact with your dog how to interact with them. You should also continue with the PREVENTION advice and disagree/provide a consequence for any aggressive/barking behaviour.

ON A WALK

To cure people reactive dogs of barking at people whilst out on a walk you need to do the same as for DOG REACTIVE DOGS i.e. walking your dog at heel on a loose lead (see PULLING ON THE LEAD) and remaining in neutral.

PEOPLE COMING INTO YOUR HOME

Any people coming into your house need to pretend that your dog is **invisible**, and wait for your dog to come to them. This includes not making eye contact with your dog.

You have a few options:

1. **Bring your dog outside the house to meet on neutral territory. Walk your dog up and down calmly ignoring the new people. Let the people enter your house first.**
2. **Use the lead in the house to open the door and invite people in (with your dog behind you).**
3. **Shut your dog in another room for 5 minutes to miss the initial excitement, make sure all the guests are sitting down, before then bringing your dog in on a lead.**

In any one of these given situations your dog should be calm at heel on a loose lead and focused on you (see PULLING ON THE LEAD). If your dog starts to bark or leave their calm state you need to take control of the situation.

You can ask for a sit and then stroke them when they are calm, or employ the snow plough away from the people (see DOG REACTIVE DOGS). Alternatively if you have dropped the lead because your dog was calm, pick it up and get your dog focused on you again/put them out of the room as a short term consequence. Repeat introductions until you end on calm behaviour.

Your dog might not want to interact with your guests, in this case the people need to respect this and continue to ignore your dog.

However, if a person visiting your house really wants to engage with your dog the best thing they might do is to turn their back to your dog (cutting down their projected energy) and sit on the floor (making themselves smaller and less threatening). It won't help if they look at your dog and try to reassure them through talking to them.

You need to be able to read your dog's body language and understand what their intentions are. If your dog is too still and silent; is barking; or maybe staring intently/exhibiting nervous eye movement; or demonstrating jerky body movements this means the meeting might not go well.

If you have ever observed children who are afraid of dogs their body language is stiff and jerky. They put their hand in to stroke the dog and then jerk it away quickly. The same is true for dogs. If a dog is unsure this will be mirrored in stiff body language.

If your dog is relaxed this will be reflected in their relaxed, fluid body language. If your dog is displaying neutral, fluid body language and they approach the person sniffing them first ... this should no doubt be a good meeting.

It is a good idea to let guests throw **treats** to your dog, or hand feed your dog if they approach the person with relaxed body language. Then to progress to **stroking** your dog **under the chin**. If they try and stroke the top of your dog's head or back your dog can feel trapped.

MUZZLES

To remove the fear factor and allow yourself to relax ... so that in turn your dog has more chance of relaxing a muzzle can be used. You can use a muzzle until you are confident you can read your dog's body language, and you can TRUST them again. You can also use a muzzle in instances where you can't instruct the people to ignore your dog, especially with young children.

You can buy comfortable, soft silicone basket muzzles suitable for eating and drinking. This is obviously a temporary solution, and muzzles should only be worn for short, supervised periods. But they can be useful if children are visiting your house, or as a tool to build back the TRUST between you and your dog.

To fit a muzzle to your dog see the PULLING ON THE LEAD chapter which includes USING HALTI STYLE LEADS - the same technique as described here can be used for a muzzle.

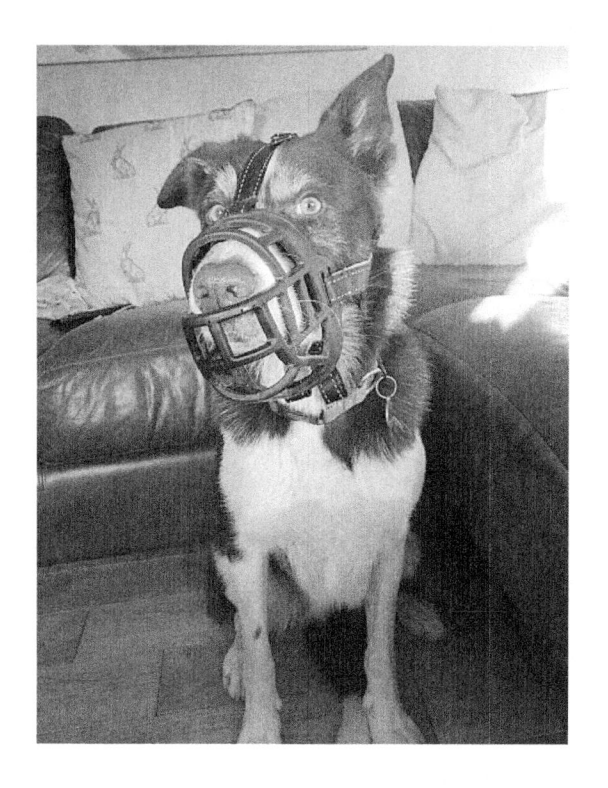

Kenny modelling a soft silicone muzzle.

NOTE - Not all muzzles of this style are soft, the silicone should be easy to manipulate.

To have a good bond with your dog you need LOVE, TRUST and RESPECT. If your dog has shown aggression towards a person in the past this will have eroded the TRUST in your relationship. However, in order for your dog to not bite anyone in the future you need to project energy which is saying "I trust this person" and "I trust you".

This might seem like a Catch 22 ... and it is. Your dog will sense when you don't TRUST them around people. This projected mistrust will most certainly hinder progress as unconsciously you are giving your dog instructions not to trust the people.

Just as when my inherently friendly dog's only instance of aggression occurred in Cyprus. He picked up on my unease in the presence of the naked hikers, and interpreted this as "don't trust these people". Your dog's reaction won't improve if they sense any mistrust from you.

HOW TO BUILD UP TRUST

Face your fears in a controlled environment. Don't be EMBARRASSED to use a muzzle so that you can relax. If you are relaxed and giving out neutral energy, your dog is more likely to stay in neutral.

Don't be afraid to use a lead inside the house. If your dog is on a short lead at your side you are in control of the situation. Once you see your dog has neutral body language you can drop the lead. Leave it dragging along the floor so that you can quickly regain control of the situation.

As soon as your dog relaxes let the lead go. Any signs of a reaction pick up the lead again. Keep repeating. The more chances your dog has to learn the faster the rehabilitation will be.

DIFFERENT TYPES OF DOGS

As discussed in the chapter on DOG REACTIVE DOGS different approaches are appropriate for different types of dogs.

The snow plough might be good for controlling more CONFIDENT or NERVOUS AGGRESSIVE dogs, moving them away from the people. But for purely fearful dogs it might better to show them there is nothing to be afraid of. Go up to the people, turn your back to them and crouch down thus encouraging your dog to come over and interact with you.

You shouldn't reassure your dog verbally or call them over. In fact you need to totally ignore your dog, but you need to communicate there isn't anything to fear by your body language and your increased proximity to the perceived threat. Remain calm and turn your back on the threat (the person). If your dog follows you over calmly stroke them.

If they remain fearful try putting them on the lead and walking at a distance with them on a short lead at your side ... again continue to remain calm and ignore the people. If they remain calm on the lead gradually decrease the distance. Reward any calm behaviour with verbal praise, stroking or treats.

THE IMPORTANCE OF TERRITORY

If your dog is aggressive towards people in the house (be they visitors or people who live in the house), reducing their territory (access to beds and sofas) can also help reduce aggression.

If your dog is exhibiting territorial behaviour toward for example their crate you need to stop them having access to this source of power for a period of time, and only re-allow access if there is no aggression displayed. Try swapping an enclosed crate for an open bed, or keep the crate closed.

Another option if your dog is becoming territorial towards their bed you need to practise removing them in a confident manner. Crouch down to their level so you aren't towering over them, but hold your ground and disagree with any growling/nipping behaviour.

If the aggression is to do with furniture you need to identify the area ... be it a particular sofa or area in the house and claim the area back by preventing your dog having access to it. Use your disagreeing noise if they enter the area, and hold your dog's collar to remove them from the area.

You need to keep removing them (maybe placing them out of the room for 1 minute), until your patience pays off and they learn if they want to stay in the room they are not allowed on the furniture.

It's up to you to find out what works best for your dog. The restriction could be total, or temporary - even sitting on your sofa and not allow your dog up for 5 minutes can help - lean forwards and push your dog down on the chest, whilst making your disagreeing noise.

You can't react emotionally, even if your dog gives you a nip ... so in extreme cases you might need to wear tough gloves.

TIP - Allowing your dog up on furniture gives your dog a larger territory, and a higher standing within the family hierarchy. Therefore to reduce your dog's power base restricting access to furniture can help reduce aggressive behaviour.

HOW TO DRY OR BRUSH YOUR DOG WITHOUT ANY AGGRESSION

There are two types of aggression - that associated with dominance and hierarchy; and fear induced aggression.

In the case of dogs who are aggressive whilst being dried or brushed it is often fear based. This is why it is always good to introduce puppies to being dried and brushed early on (many groomers offer puppy taster sessions for this very reason).

In the instance of nervous aggression you have three options:

- Turn the fear into excitement.
- Remain relaxed, calm and confident to demonstrate there is nothing to fear.
- Create a new association with the fear using treats.

In chapter 2 I described how you can used excitement to overcome your dog's fear of getting into the car. In this instance excitement works far better than treats.

However, in some situations treats are more appropriate to use to provide a new association. For instance new people coming into your house, or while drying your dog with a towel or brushing them.

If your dog has already bitten you whilst attempting to dry or brush them you need to either get them comfortable wearing a muzzle, or wear thick gloves to take the FEAR away. Then proceed as follows.

- Claim the towel or brush by placing it on the floor and getting your dog to move away (just as in the COMMUNICATION EXERCISE).
- Hold your dog's collar under their chin (it's harder for them to bite you here) and start to towel or brush their feet followed by their body for a few seconds at a time.
- Ask someone else to simultaneously feed your dog very small treats.

This should be done little and often to create a new association with being brushed and dried. The towel and brushes are yours, and you need to disagree with a noise if your dog tries to mouth them.

6. CHILD REACTIVE DOGS

Within our own families our dogs perceive a hierarchy exists. Children are naturally loving and generally don't project assertive energy. This can automatically put them in a dog's eyes as near the bottom of the family hierarchy, or at least on a par with your dog who might view them as they would their own siblings.

In canine society it is acceptable to nip and growl at litter mates, but not at parent dogs.

HOW A YOUR DOG MIGHT SEE THE FAMILY HIERARCHY

- **TOP** - PARENTS - LOVE, TRUST, RESPECT
- **MIDDLE** - DOG/CHILDREN
- **BOTTOM** - CHILDREN - LOVE, LOVE, LOVE

When children enter a dog's personal space, especially those who are either naturally CONFIDENT or perhaps a bit NERVOUS, they may get a negative reaction. This can be in the form of a growl or a nip, or in the worst case a significant bite.

Dogs prefer neutral balance. If one dog in a group is displaying signs of anxiety or aggression, then the others will confront the offending dog to restore the status quo. Thus, children who naturally are more excitable or nervous around dogs are projecting unbalanced energy … and are also more likely to ignite a reaction.

PREVENTION

To prevent your dog becoming reactive around children they need to be socialised, and acclimatised to children's intense energy. Dogs who are handled by children from a young age will learn to be more tolerant than those who are not.

If you don't have children in your house (or even if you do) it's a good idea to associate grabbing of tails, ears and paws with food rewards. Hold food inside a closed fist and allow your dog to lick at the food while you stroke them firmly, or a little grabby like a young child would. Gradually release the food as you continue to handle your dog's sensitive areas a little roughly.

Of course it depends on the individual dog, and even some dogs who are brought up with children can still turn and react if provoked. This is why you also need to make sure that the children respect a dog's personal space. Dogs who are natural COMMUNICATORS will generally also be more tolerant of children, than those who are born CONFIDENT or NERVOUS.

CURE

If your dog does react towards a child then the response from you should be instantaneous in your disagreement. You should be the higher ranking leader and can set the rules. You need to make your noise indicating disagreement "shhh" or a command word in a low growly voice. **Your energy has to match your dogs, otherwise you risk being ignored.**

If appropriate also immediately remove the dog from a situation ... for example if you are all on the sofa then your dog doesn't get to stay there. This consequence should only be short lived, thereby giving your dog lots of chances to learn.

You can try and increase a child's standing in the hierarchy by including them in your dogs training and feeding routine (providing your dog doesn't display food guarding behaviour). For instance this can be as simple as a child asking for a "sit" before feeding your dog their meal.

You also need to provide rules and boundaries for the children, not just your dog. You need to ensure that children respect your dog's personal space.

Getting children to sit still and calmly throw high value treats to your dog, and not to try and pet them can help your dog to make a new association. Children should only stroke your dog if your dog approaches them with relaxed fluid body motions. It can help a NERVOUS dog relax if the children stroke them from under the chin.

My kids used to like picking up our cockapoo when he was puppy, but as he grew older I had to enforce a new rule that stipulated they didn't pick him up. He had started growling when they picked him up I think as he no longer felt safe. My kids also aren't allowed to handle the dogs' bones, dogs will naturally food guard against lower ranking members of the family. Some dogs will also toy guard.

In the case of very young children who don't understand boundaries, then if you have any doubts ensure your dog is never left unsupervised with a young child or consider the short term use of a comfortable muzzle.

7. CAT/SMALL PET REACTIVE DOGS

Cats can make very good leaders, and often with one swipe of their paw they can achieve this status!

PREVENTION

Introducing puppies to cats, or other small pets is the best way to prevent your dog becoming pet reactive. Vice versa it will also be easier to bond a young animal such as a kitten with an adult dog, than to bond to an adult animal to an adult dog.

Alternatively, an older rescue dog with low prey drive, would be a good addition to any household already containing a cat or small pets.

CURE

You have introduced a new dog into your household which already contains a cat or small pet, and this dog is desperate to play chase!

There are various methods you can employ to initially introduce your dog to the other pets:

- Place an adult cat in a crate, or hold a kitten or other small pet in your arms (you might want to ask someone to help you).
- Ask your dog for a "sit" or "lie down", hold the crate or pet over the dog. If your dog makes a move ... disagree with your chosen noise, and use your projected energy and intention to ask your dog to calm down.
- If this doesn't work, the next stage is to lie your dog on their side, and repeat the above exercise. This exercise is not to be used in other situations ... only with small, defenceless animals (this can include very small puppies).

- OR - Place your dog on a 2-3 meter training lead and use a head collar muzzle to direct your dog's head away from the cat whilst using your disagreeing noise (see REHABILITATION in DOG REACTIVE DOGS).

After initial introductions you might want to utilise the following for dog/cat relationships ... until you fully TRUST your dog:

- Keep the cat and dog separated by a door, and then progress to a stair gate.
- Have your dog on the lead within the house to prevent chasing.
- Muzzle your dog for a short period when first introduced to the cat off the lead.

CASE STUDY

EDDIE'S FRIENDS

Whilst living in Cyprus I adopted a stray kitten who was abandoned outside my house. I only became aware of the kitten's presence when Eddie ran like crazy barking towards a hedge.

I then discovered and rescued the kitten from the depths of the shrubbery, and brought her inside. I utilised the aforementioned method with Eddie and the stray kitten. The kitten had found a home and was to become known as Mocha.

I asked Eddie for a "sit" and held Mocha over him. With Eddie being a natural COMMUNICATOR he didn't react aggressively, and I didn't need to progress to the next stage of lying him on his side. Within 10 minutes he had accepted and was playing with Mocha.

As our family grew to include two pet tortoises I employed the same method successfully ... and it even worked on the wild chameleon who used to visit my garden - for some reason I christened the chameleon "Gary"!

Eddie with Mocha and below with Gary.

8. NIPPING

PREVENTION & CURE

To prevent your puppy turning nipping into a long term problem try the following:

- **Freeze** and stop moving your hands the instance you are nipped. Stay calm, **don't react** and by keeping still you are avoiding turning the nipping into a game. If you are finding this hard - consider wearing leather gloves when handling your puppy. Also, **making your hand into a fist can be a good idea** ... still fists are harder to chew than wiggly fingers! **Only resume stroking your puppy when the nipping has stopped.**
- **Yelp** - as one of their litter mates would to indicate pain. A loud yelp ... even when you aren't in pain ... can stop a puppy in their tracks.

- If this doesn't work some puppies will stop the instant you do a deep **growl and lean towards them.** Just as a mother dog might growl if one of her pups causes her pain whilst suckling.
- **Send a message** to your puppy by holding their collar (under their chin with your hand in a fist - it is harder for them to nip you here) keeping them still and then releasing (or stroke their head from behind - don't come in from the front as this provides another target) them the second they calm down/stop trying to bite you. This sends a clear message ... you are free to go (or get affection) only when you stop being over excited and nippy.
- Hold a **chew** or **dog toy** in your hand to **redirect the nipping** onto the object.
- You might try removing your puppy out of the room as a **consequence** of nipping, but just for a very short period. Repeat. This method can be helpful when children are involved, and for puppies who have already turned nipping their owners fingers into a game.

- You might also try combining your **disagreeing noise**, with **firmly pushing** your puppy **away** from you. Push your puppy away on their chest as demonstrated in the COMMUNICATION EXERCISE. You need to claim your personal space, but remember to stay calm.

TIP - If a puppy tries to nibble your fingers - make a fist and keep your hand still.

TIP - Hold a chew to redirect chewing.

TIP - If your puppy has already turned nipping into a game, you need to put them out of the room for a short time as a consequence.

9. FOOD AND TOY GUARDING

It is natural for dogs to guard their food and possessions, rather than share them.

PREVENTION

In order for your dog not to food or resource guard around humans it's important to practise calmly removing and returning food and toys from an early age. It's a good idea to practise exchanging the food for a higher value treat, thus ensuring your dog sees the benefits.

Lift your dog's food bowl directly up from the floor, give your dog a treat in return. Hold the bowl mid-air for a couple of seconds before returning it. You aren't pulling it away towards yourself, you are lifting up and holding your ground.

It's also useful to be able to take away an edible chew. Hold your hand still, don't pull away and give the "leave it" command. You can give a treat at this point. Wait a few seconds before also returning the chew as an additional reward.

It is natural for dogs to food guard with other dogs, especially new dogs. To prevent any clashes occurring when you have another dog visiting you might be wise to remove any edible chews (plus possibly toys).

CURE

1. FOOD

Your dog has become possessive, and more dominant than you when around food. You need to show them the benefits of giving up their food. In order to do this you need to be calm, yet confident and take away the FEAR factor.

There are some basket muzzles which allow dogs to eat whilst wearing them. If you can get your dog to wear one of these this will take away the FEAR, and allow you to remain calm. See the section in chapter 2 USING HALTI STYLE LEADS - the same principles apply to get your dog used to wearing a muzzle.

If your dog does nip you, remember you can't show any emotion or even react! You still need to hold your ground and continue calmly. In order to do this without the use of a muzzle you might consider wearing tough gloves.

If the problem is very bad and you own a big dog it might be advisable to also have someone holding your dog on a lead.

STOP FOOD GUARDING

- Use a low value man-made hollow bone or toy to offer to your dog.
- Lure your dog away with a trail of high value small treats placed on the floor in a line about 1 metre long.

- The split second your dog drops the hollow bone and starts eating the treats verbally praise them.
- Work towards picking up the low value object for a second or two, and then put it down in the same place. If any growling occurs disagree using your noise.

Repeat the above exercise with peanut butter added to the interior of the bone. Keep upgrading the value of the bone until your dog learns they aren't going to loose out when you take food away from them.

You can try the same exercise with your dogs food bowl, starting with low value kibble in the bowl, and high value chicken or sausage to lure your dog away.

To cure food bowl aggression **hand feeding** your dog their meals for an extended length of time should also help.

You can also practise doing a **straight swap**. Give your dog a low value bone, ask for a "leave it", give your dog a treat, before immediately returning the bone.

TIP - Place your dog's food bowl on a step ... this elevation makes less likely your dog will act possessively.

2. TOYS

When taking a toy off your dog the main thing you need to do is ... **hold your hand still.**

You need to have mastered the COMMUNICATION EXERCISE in order to successfully claim toys from your dog. The principle is the same - hold your hand still, hold your ground and ask your dog to move away. Instinctively you will want to pull your hand towards you ... but you are going to do the opposite and hold your ground, thus claiming the toy.

If you move your hand around you might also initiating a fun game of tug of war!

You need to communicate the same message as with food guarding - you will get rewarded for giving up the toy. Give your dog a **treat** when they give you the toy, also **give them their toy back** after a few seconds as an additional reward.

You can also practise the "LEAVE IT" COMMAND and follow the advice in the STEALING OBJECTS chapter.

10. FUSSY EATERS

PREVENTION

To prevent your dog from becoming a fussy eater - remain calm at meal times, and don't leave the food bowl on the floor for more than **5 minutes**.

If your dog is ever not hungry don't try and tempt them with other types of food. There maybe a reason why your dog isn't eating, they might have an upset stomach. Missing one meal won't harm your dog (if a longer term loss of appetite occurs then you need to take your dog to the vets).

If you continue to feed your dog different foods in an attempt to get them to eat, you might teach them to refuse their usual food.

Asking your dog to "sit" and "wait" can be a good routine to get into before feeding ... giving you space and RESPECT.

CURE

To cure your dog from being a fussy eater, apply all the advice from the PREVENTION section ... plus some additional steps:

- Take your dog for a **walk** before feeding them.
- Try feeding them just **once/day** for a short period (adult dogs only).
- Don't PITY them, remain calm and remove any uneaten food after **5 minutes**.

Unless your dog is suffering from a medical condition affecting their appetite there is no reason why they shouldn't eat food that they have previously eaten. Remember dogs read your energy and will pick up if you PITY them.

11. STEALING FOOD

PREVENTION & CURE

The following exercise can both PREVENT dogs stealing food, and CURE dogs from stealing food. It is also a great way to learn how to project your energy to disagree with your dog - and in essence is the same as the COMMUNICATION EXERCISE - the only difference being that we now use human food (for a short period only so as not to encourage begging) instead of dog treats.

If you get angry with your dog when you catch them stealing food ... it may just encourage them to do it when you leave the room. If you practise the following exercise this will help you claim the food as your own.

STOP STEALING FOOD EXERCISE

- Crouch down to be at your dog's level.
- Hold a plain biscuit (or any human dog safe food) out in front of you in one hand, and in the other hand have some smaller pieces of food. This is the only time when I don't use dog treats or high value meat as a reward. This is due to the message we are going to communicate about human food.
- When your dog attempts to lick/sniff/eat the food you are going to nudge them away with your free hand, simultaneously making your chosen noise. Most people naturally draw back the biscuit. But this is the challenge ... to **hold your space** and to use your energy and intention to ask your dog to move away.
- The instant your dog moves back and looks away or at you, you are going to give them a piece of the biscuit from your other hand.
- The next stage is to leave food at **coffee table** height, ask your dog to leave it alone using your noise, and then throw them some food as a reward.

Thus, you are communicating the message - leave that alone and you will get rewarded. In the future instead of getting ANGRY with your dog you can disagree with them using your noise.

NOTE - This cure might only work when you are in the house. My dogs won't touch food when I am home, even if I leave the room. However, the minute I walk out the front door any food within reach appears to be fair game. Thus, I have learned to my cost not to leave food out when I'm not there ... my son's 5th birthday cake has been our biggest casualty to date!

12. STEALING OBJECTS

PREVENTION AND CURE

Most puppies love nothing better than to get hold of something they shouldn't! How you react will determine if this turns into a fun game and entrenched habit, or if you can prevent your dog from repeating this behaviour.

You need to remain CALM, and not get ANGRY. Getting ANGRY will increase the energy of the situation and maybe the fun for your dog. A young, excitable puppy might feed off your FRUSTRATION and ANGER. Alternatively, they might just steal objects behind your back.

Remember not to chase after your dog:

- Try ignoring them initially. Walk out of the room and wait for your dog to follow. Bend down with your back to them. They may well come over to you out of curiosity.
- You can calmly grab hold of your dog's collar, and then the object in your dog's mouth. Freeze your hand still, and use the "leave it" command.
- Replace the object with one of your dog's own toys (or give your dog their own toy back if you are using it as a training exercise).

If ignoring your dog doesn't work, then you need to try other tactics:

- Use your disagreeing noise from a distance to encourage your dog to drop the item.
- Ask your dog to "wait" and go over to them to retrieve the object ("leave it").
- Again, replace the object with one of your dog's toys and then praise them.
- OR - enact a consequence such as being put out of the room, outside or in their crate for a few minutes might work.

BEWARE OF COMMUNICATING THE WRONG MESSAGE

I have had clients with dogs who have had possessive guarding tendencies towards objects in their mouth, so as discussed in the food guarding chapter they have exchanged the object (often the TV remote!) for a treat. The only problem is that this has encouraged their dog to continue to steal the remote.

Firstly if you catch your dog sniffing the object they like to steal, in this case the remote, use your disagreeing noise to prevent them stealing it in the first place.

A good exercise can be to put the remote on the floor and claim it as yours. Use your noise (and a nudge out of the way if your dog doesn't listen) to keep your dog away from it.

Alternatively, if you are out of the room and discover they have picked up the remote ask for a "leave it" to rescue it, and then immediately replace it with one of your dog's toys and praise them verbally.

You need to be 100% consistent, and demonstrate more patience than your dog.

Cesar racing round very proudly with his own toy. If I hadn't given him his own toys, and praised him ... he would have continued to steal my children's teddies.

13. GENERAL ANXIETY AND FIREWORKS

PREVENTION AND CURE

With generalised anxiety PREVENTION and CURE are one and the same. Certain breeds and dogs who are born naturally NERVOUS alarm barkers are more likely to suffer from anxiety.

A NERVOUS dog needs to have a CONFIDENT owner, who communicates through confident body language that there is nothing to be afraid of.

It should be remembered that in this instance dogs are different from children. To reassure a scared child they need soft words and perhaps a hug. To similarly reassure and stroke an unbalanced dog is to positively reinforce the fearful or anxious behaviour.

The best way you can reassure your dog is through your own confident body language and close proximity, but to only stroke them the split second they themselves are calm.

CALM CONFIDENCE CAN ALLAY FEAR

On nights when firework displays are occurring any dog might legitimately be scared, this is when your confidence can help reassure your dog. It's obviously a good idea to try and drown out the noise, but when the noise of the fireworks penetrates that of the television you might need to intervene.

Try holding your dog's collar, breathing deeply and remaining physically relaxed. Your confidence and reassuring presence should transfer to your dog, all without uttering a word.

Once your dog is also relaxed and demonstrating neutral body language, you can gently stroke them as praise. This reward rather than telling your dog "good boy" or "girl" will reinforce that you want them to be calm and *not* fearful.

Alternatively, if you do want to talk to your dog make sure your voice is calm, confident and monotone to convey calm energy.

TURNING FEAR INTO EXCITEMENT

Fear is closely related to excitement, and in some cases this similarity in emotions can be used to turn hesitancy into excitement. Some dogs might respond better on Bon Fire Night if you get them excited to over come their fear.

My cockapoo used to be scared of squeaky gates. Initially I got him super excited and ran through the gate with him, until he was no longer fearful and we could walk normally through any gate.

Sometimes dogs need words of encouragement in a higher voice, or the situation may need you to say absolutely nothing. You need to use your intuition as to what is required.

CASE STUDY

Cesar used to bark when new people came into a tiny park we often visit. Instead of calling him to me I would walk over to the people, and turn my back to them. I then proceeded to crouch down, but would continue to ignore my NERVOUS dog.

I had remained calm, and turned my back on the threat to demonstrate there was nothing to fear. By bending down I was communicating I wanted my dog to come over (see POOR RECALL), but by ignoring him I wasn't putting any pressure on him to do so.

In every instance Cesar came over to me and ended up relaxed and happily sniffing the new people. I hadn't needed to say a word to my dog ... as my body language had done all the talking!

14. SEPARATION ANXIETY

It is natural for a pack or family of dogs to be together all the time, so sometimes one of the hardest lessons for a dog to learn is to be separated from the group.

PREVENTION

Some breeds are particularly likely to suffer from separation anxiety, including the poodle, cocker and King Charles spaniels. However, lower energy breeds such as the pug, French bulldog, and basset hound are less prone to it (note - flat faced breeds are often better crossed to avoid associated breathing problems).

Whichever breed you end up with you can work on preventing your dog from developing separation anxiety. The best thing you can do to prevent your dog from suffering with separation anxiety, is to make sure you **leave them alone for short periods from the very beginning.** This slowly conditions your dog to being left alone.

You can't PITY your puppy or new dog, you just need to see it as part of their training. Start by leaving the room closing the door behind you, and then returning a few seconds later ... as if nothing has happened.

Ignore (including no eye contact) your dog when you leave, and ignore them on your return whatever their behaviour. You are teaching an important message ... there is no big deal about being left. Do this little and often, and soon your dog will remain in neutral ... just as you do.

Separation anxiety can occur not just when you leave the house, but also within the house. If your dog is used to coming everywhere with you as a puppy, it can be hard when you ask them to spend time away from you. That's why it's best to start as you mean to go on.

The same applies for leaving the house. It would even be a good idea to do the same exercise as you would leaving a room ... but actually to leave the house for very short periods. This way your dog gradually gets used to being left alone.

CURE

Your dog suffers with separation anxiety when you leave them. It can either be within the house or when you leave the house.

It should be noted that getting another dog probably won't solve the problem, as your dog is being left in an unbalanced state due to being apart from you.

There are in actual fact two ways of taking your leave from your dog. As always different methods work better for different dogs:

- When you take your leave from them settle them in their **bed**, no talking is required but gentle stroking might help. Once your dog is calm stand in front of them and hold your ground for a minute and possibly issue a firm **"wait"** command, before calmly walking away. **Don't look back**. Just leave quietly. On your return again ignore your dog until they are calm. You are illustrating to your dog there is nothing to get emotional about when you leave or return. By staying in neutral, your dog is more likely to follow your lead.
- **Do nothing**. Simply totally **ignore** your dog wherever they may be in the house - no looking, talking or emotional energy directed towards them - as you calmly walk out of the door.

Once you have conditioned your dog to your leaving, you can start leaving them for longer periods. Before doing this to give your dog the best chance of success, take them for a **long walk** to burn off any excessive energy which can fuel their anxiety. A tired dog should find it easier to settle down for a nap whilst their family is away.

TIP - If your dog tries to follow you when you leave, use the first method whereby you settle them in their bed and ask for a "wait".

You might want to leave your dog in their crate (see CRATE TRAINING) or in a room where they can do the least damage. Don't PITY your dog, as they will read your energy and this will only make the separation anxiety worse. If you are leaving your dog in their crate, you need to have done enough crate training for them to be relaxed when you shut them in.

Another strategy is **distraction** ... try leaving an interactive toy with a food element. Dogs won't eat when they are stressed, but if your dog is a foodie it might be worth a try. A dispensing ball filled with tiny pieces of carrot and/or dog treats might work well, or peanut butter licked off an indented tray or ball.

There isn't always a quick fix for separation anxiety, you need to be patient. Over time your dog will follow your lead and realise what you are asking of them. For naturally NERVOUS dogs it can be a common problem for them to suffer from separation anxiety. It might take a while for their confidence to build, but persevere and you both will be rewarded.

If am leaving my cockapoo in the house when other people are home, they have told me he doesn't whine if I have told him to "wait", but will whine a little if I just leave without saying anything. I think he likes to know I am coming back so he can relax properly.

15. POOR TRAVELLERS

If your dog has a bad experience travelling in the car they can associate travel with stress. This stress can be reflected in anxious barking, excessive salivating or shaking.

Alternatively they might just be over stimulated whilst travelling in the car.

PREVENTION

To prevent your new dog having a bad experience in the car the following tips can be helpful:

- Reassure your dog initially by letting them travel within reach of you, and if possible have another person driving. If there isn't anyone available to act as your chauffeur ... then the next best thing is to have your dog on the front seat next to you. Dog harness seat belts are a great idea to keep your dog safe, or a small travel bag that can be strapped in.

- Go on short journeys initially to take your dog to a fun place ... the best fun is obviously to go on a walk.

CASE STUDY

My cockapoo as a youngster was travelling in the boot of my car, when as puppies are prone to do he vomited due to travel sickness. The very next time he travelled in the car, I noticed that he was excessively drooling. I realised he was associating being sick that one time with car travel in general.

My intuition told me he needed reassurance. The next time we took a journey, I asked my 9 year old daughter to hold him on her knee in the front passenger seat. This produced the same result ... lots of drool.

My next attempt to reassure Cesar was successful. I asked my husband to drive, and I sat in the front with Cesar in his favourite place, zipped up inside my winter coat with just his head poking out. He remained perfectly relaxed, and I didn't even need to wash my coat as there was no drool!

Cesar like many cockapoos has bonded to one person in particular (me). He therefore takes his reassurance from me, and to this day still often travels shotgun.

NOTE - Cesar will also travel well in the boot of my car in a covered crate. This is a less stimulating place for dogs to travel and can reduce excited whining or barking.

CURE

TIPS FOR IMPROVED TRAVEL EXPERIENCES

- For **over excited dogs** you need a **calm approach** to the car, for **fearful dogs** you need to get them **excited before entering** the car to over come their fear (see DOGS WHO WON'T WALK ON THE LEAD/USE STAIRS/JUMP INTO THE CAR). If your dog is over excited before they enter the car you need to walk your dog at heel (see PULLING ON THE LEAD) backwards and forwards to the car, until they can approach calmly. Don't enter the car until your dog is calm.
- For barking in the car, you might need to disagree with this behaviour. Try using your noise and possibly giving a gentle tug on your dogs' collar, or changing their position of travel to remove any visual triggers. N.B. If your dog is whining with pure excitement it can be difficult to stop this, and probably pointless to try.

- **As well as using excitement to over come fear, you can also spend time in the car with the doors open, and don't go anywhere.** Having the doors open will stop your dog feeling trapped. I did this with a rescue border collie cross we had when I was a teenager. He had been found near a motorway, and was terrified of cars. I also fed him treats in the stationary car, but only after he had settled down.
- I then progressed to going **short journeys of less than 5 minutes** to go on a walk ... if possible with someone else driving. If your dog starts getting anxious, fast stroking and talking to your dog can act as a distraction, and turn their focus on to you. However, all dogs are different, you might not need to say a word, and just be there as a confident quiet presence.
- Some dogs may feel more secure in a **covered crate**, this can also stop your dog barking in the car at visual triggers.

All dogs are individuals, and it's worth experimenting to allow your dog to experience stress free travel.

16. EXCESSIVE BARKING

There is obviously no CURE for barking. However, there are certain things you can do to prevent the problem getting worse, and to reduce excessive barking within the house.

PREVENTION

Dogs do learn by example, so if your present dog is noisy in the house and this is a problem for you ... make sure you wait before adding another dog to your family.

If you are thinking of getting a puppy consider breeds who are not so vocal. This includes the whippet, greyhound, basenji, saluki or French bulldog (French bulldog crosses will avoid associated breathing problems with flat faced dogs).

If you get ANGRY when your dog barks, your intense energy will simply add fuel to the fire. You can raise your voice to match the intensity of the barking to issue a command, but if you do so in ANGER you risk the chance of it back firing.

To prevent your dog barking at the doorbell, a knock at the door or the bang of a letter box ... you can desensitise your dog to the noise. With a puppy, or new dog it's worth repeating the exercise of feeding them treats, whilst simultaneously making the aforementioned noises.

I have observed two general types of barking:

1. WORRIED BARKING - where the dog hears or sees something, but generally doesn't rush towards the trigger to defend their territory. Instead they sound the **alarm** and issue a worried sounding bark.

2. CONFIDENT TERRITORIAL BARKING - whereby a dog rushes to a window or door and barks in an effort to **defend** their territory.

Prevention is always easier than cure. A highly agitated dog is always harder to deal with than a dog who hasn't reached those heights. There are different pre-emptive approaches for stopping your dog barking.

You notice your dog's body language changing - their ears are pricked up, they are looking alert and you know they are just about to bark ... now is the time to intervene.

APPROACH ONE

RECALL AND DISTRACTION – FOR TERRITORIAL/CONFIDENT & WORRIED BARKERS

- **Call** your dog to you or if your dog's recall is poor (see POOR RECALL) then go over to them ... in both instances then hold their collar.
- Keep hold of their **collar** and either wait until they become calm by doing nothing, *or* ask for a "sit" to distract them. You might need to give a gentle tug on their collar, or click your fingers/make a squeaking/kissing noise with your lips to get their attention focused on you ... before asking for the "sit".
- **Stroke** them when they are calm, no verbal praise required.

APPROACH TWO

DISAGREEMENT – FOR TERRITORIAL CONFIDENT BARKERS ONLY

- For dogs who bark territorially ... disagree using your noise, before the barking even starts. This probably won't work for more NERVOUS worried barkers, who need distraction rather than disagreement.
- Use voice control to move your dog away from the area that is causing them to become alert. Perhaps sending them on their bed, or out of the room.

CURE

You aren't always there to prevent your dog reaching high intensity barking. Sometimes you need to step in, and stop the barking when your dog is going full pelt.

One suggestion to stop this happening too often, is to make sure you keep your dog within a manageable area. Very obvious but by shutting a few doors you can keep your dog within a smaller area, which allows you to be on hand to prevent the barking escalating.

The tactics change slightly when your dog is already mid-bark:

WORRIED BARKING

Same as in PREVENTION (RECALL AND DISTRACTION) – but sometimes I also use faster stroking to distract a NERVOUS barker mid-bark. Plus, talking to them in an excited way can turn their fear into excitement … this also distracts the dog by diverting their focus onto you. Then when the dog has calmed down (a good sign is when their body is still, or perhaps when they sit or lie down) I gently stroke them with no verbal praise.

I found treats as a distraction didn't work with NERVOUS dogs, but rather made their barking worse. They were being directly rewarded for the behaviour I was trying to prevent. However, toys can work as a good distraction.

CONFIDENT TERRITORIAL BARKERS

For more confident territorial barkers you might need a different approach. They can't always be distracted, in which case you need to disagree with the behaviour. There are a few methods that can be tried.

HOLDING THE COLLAR

- As mentioned in PREVENTION you can hold your dog's collar until they stop barking. You might want to do this before asking for a "sit", or try giving a couple of gentle tugs on your dog's collar combined with your disagreeing noise. This will gain their attention and bring them back down to neutral.
- Once neutral body language is achieved, keep hold of the collar and with your other hand calmly stroke your dog.

SENDING AWAY

Sending your dog out of the room or onto their bed (see BED in COMMANDS). If your dog is barking at full volume, then your energy needs to equal their intensity. You will need to raise your voice, but not in ANGER and use a command to move them away from the stimulus.

SNOW PLOUGH

- You can use the snow plough maneuver to claim an area/object that your dog is intensely barking at. This can be achieved by coming in front of them with your back to the stimulus for example the window, and driving them away. For larger dogs you may have to gently nudge the dog with your knees, you basically need to keep walking even if your dog doesn't get out of the way ... hence the "snow plough".
- Keep your hands on your hips or behind your back to prevent larger dogs nipping your hands when they are in an intense state. Dogs can nip when they are highly agitated to release energy. This is not a pre-meditated action and shouldn't be taken personally if your dog behaves in this way.
- Click your fingers (or give a gentle tug on your dog's collar) then ask for a "sit", before gently stroking them as a reward for neutral - a still and relaxed body ... including the tail.

NOTE - After a period of time of consistently using the snow plough, you should be able to stop using it and only use voice control.

BARKING AT THE TV

Even if your dog is sitting next to you on the sofa and barking at the telly ... ensure they are sitting on the side of you furthest away from the TV to have the best chance of them listening to you. Then follow the steps for HOLDING THE COLLAR.

Alternatively, if you have failed to stop your dog barking at the telly and they have been able to get near to the stimulus ... employ the **snow plough** or **send them out of the room** as a short term consequence.

TIP - Make sure you are in between the stimulus and your dog (with your back to the stimulus) claim the area and stop them barking.

RESTRICTED ACCESS

If your dog always sits on one particular chair to bark out of the window, access to this chair should be restricted. Your dog should either not be allowed on the chair, or only when someone else is occupying the chair.

DESENSITISE YOUR DOG TO NOISE

If your dog has imprinted learned behaviour to a certain sound, it may take a very long time to desensitise them to that noise, and you may well be onto a losing battle.

Prevention is far easier that cure, that is why it is worth desensitising puppies and new dogs to noises (or even worth doing with your dog if you move house). But, if you have a dog obsessed by barking at your letter box ... the simplest solution may just be to get an outside letter box.

As regards to knocking on the door ... refer to the next section JUMPING UP to look for WAYS TO STOP YOUR DOG GETTING EXCITED WHEN VISITORS ARRIVE.

17. JUMPING UP

PREVENTION

If you have ever observed a therapy dog in training, you might have noticed members of the public are only allowed to stroke them when they have all four paws on the floor. A dog who gets attention with all four paws on the floor, and ignored when they jump up ... will learn it's not beneficial to jump.

This is especially important with larger dogs. Before getting interested in dog behaviour, I used to shout in ANGER at my border collie when he jumped up at visitors ... all I did was make the problem worse!

CURE

My collie also used to jump up at me. This was an easier problem to fix than trying to stop him jumping at visitors. After a few days of turning my back to him when he jumped, and bending down to give affection whenever I saw him lying/siting down he stopped jumping up at me.

This tactic might not work with all dogs, so you could also try literally walking through the jump whilst paying no attention to your dog. Then as soon as the jumping stops lower yourself down to your dog's level and give quiet affection.

Alternatively, you can disagree with the jumping (a technique suited to when your dog jumps up at you, but maybe not so good for visitors).

Cesar used to jump all over me when I got his lead out to go on a walk. He hardly ever does this after I tried the following:

- **Lean towards** your dog and make your **disagreeing noise** the split second they jump. You may also want to follow this up by asking for a **"sit"**, before silently stroking your dog. If a "sit" is slow in coming a gentle tug on your dog's collar will help to gain their attention.
- By holding the lead in your hand and deliberately shaking it, and disagreeing every time a jump occurs you can quickly stop the jumping.

- Repeat lots of times within a short space of time. When your dog settles on the floor put the lead on, and give praise through quiet stroking.

You can use this same method to encourage your dog to jump by patting your body, and then leaning forward and making your noise when your dog jumps up ... it's much more effective than saying "get down" ... your dog understands what you mean without you even touching them. Once they have all four paws on the floor you can praise your dog by stroking them.

This exercise might sound counter-intuitive, and confusing for your dog ... asking for a jump and then saying no don't do it! But in actual fact it can be a quick way to communicate to your dog not to jump up. Some dogs just don't get it when you ignore them.

It can also be beneficial if you direct your gaze up away from your dog, and keep your hands still ... even better remove them from reach.

On muddy walks when I don't want my cockapoo to jump all over me, I make sure my hands and eyes are in the right position. When he races towards me possibly looking for a muddy cuddle, my hands are already either behind my back, or holding onto his lead around my neck ... out of his sight and reach for jumping towards. My eyes are looking away from him, angled upwards rather than downwards.

Your hands and eyes/faces are sources of energy and excitement for dogs, and one of the main things they are jumping up to interact with.

This is why conversely in achieving good recall it helps if you bend down with your arms open. You are lowering your face to within easy reach of your dog, and offering your hands ... a wonderful source of excitement and affection!

WAYS TO STOP YOUR DOG GETTING EXCITED WHEN VISITORS ARRIVE

PROVIDE A LOW ENERGY MEETING

To avoid all the excitement of the initial meeting shut your dog in their crate (with a cover over if in the same room as you), or in another room for the first 5 minutes. Make sure everyone is seated and calm before letting your dog enter the room. You might then want to employ some additional techniques - have your dog on a lead, or remove them from the room as a consequence of jumping.

CONSEQUENCE

Providing a consequence to jumping up. As soon as your dog jumps up, calmly hold their collar and remove them from the room (or hold their collar and ask for a sit). Wait a few minutes until they are calm ... let them back in (or release them from the sit). Repeat the process until your dog learns if they want to stay with the humans ... they need to be calm. You could also try sending your dog onto, and then releasing them from their bed or crate. Repetition is key, giving your dog lots of chances to learn.

USE THE LEAD

Use the lead in the house. Don't rush. Keep a lead by the door and put it on before the visitor enters. Lead your dog in front of you, away from the door giving space. Make sure you move to the other side of the room, allowing the visitor to claim the space you have given.

Ask your dog to stay by your side on a short lead, or if they are going really ballistic initiate the snowplough manoeuvre. Your dog should in this case remain behind you ... separated by your body from the visitor. As soon as your dog is in neutral drop the lead, leaving it to drag along the floor. If your dog gets too excited again, stand on or pick up the lead and repeat.

NOTE - An alternative to the snow plough is to hold your dogs collar, give a gentle tug whilst asking for a "sit". Followed again by silent stroking once your dog is calm.

It will also help if you can be firm, yet polite in asking for your visitors' help. They need to pretend your dog is **invisible** ... unless your dog calmly approaches them asking for affection. It will aid your dog if visitors can crouch down and stroke your dog on a lower level. Even eye contact from a guest will encourage a dog to jump up.

18. STALKING LAWN MOWERS, VACUUM CLEANERS ETC

PREVENTION

It's great to desensitise your puppy or new dog to loud noises. Before doing the following exercise your puppy needs to be introduced to the noise of a vacuum cleaner or lawn mower gradually. Switch the device on for a few seconds, remain calm and either totally ignore the noise or give your puppy some treats.

Only when your dog is happy with the noise should you attempt the VACUUM EXERCISE. Obviously you can do the exercise with a mop or brush straight away. As with all lessons they need to be repeated regularly to prevent your dog from forgetting.

VACUUM EXERCISE

- If your dog shows any interest in the moving item ... perform a dead **stop** and become a statue.
- Don't move away, hold your space. Simultaneously make your disagreeing noise.
- If necessary claim the mop, or whatever item you are holding by standing in front of it and moving your dog away with your energy/voice control.

CURE

To stop your dog chasing vacuum cleaners etc do the same exercise as outlined in the PREVENTION section.

If the VACUUM EXERCISE doesn't work try introducing the lead:

- If your dog still doesn't stop barking or attacking the mop ... then put them on the **lead** - probably a traditional collar and lead or slip lead for larger dogs, and a front fastening harness for smaller dogs harness. Walk up and down and keep them next to, not in front of you.
- Any significant reaction e.g. a lunge or a bark, stop or switch off the machine, lean towards your dog (bending at the waist) and disagree with your noise. Repeat.

One of my clients had an avid vacuum cleaner chaser/barker, after we put her dog on the lead and disagreed with him just a few times ... she was pleasantly surprised:

"I was so pleased to be able to hoover without having a fight! I never thought that would happen."

19. HYPERACTIVE OR OBSESSIVE DOGS

PREVENTION

With a new dog always make sure you reward them for doing nothing. Whatever the main characteristic of your dog is be it NERVOUS, a COMMUNICATOR or CONFIDENT all dogs will benefit from the positive reinforcement of calm behaviour.

This is achieved by quietly stroking your dog when they are relaxed. Stop the stroking if they react in excitement, recommence when your dog is calm ... this is called The Nothing Exercise.

It's also important to ensure your dog is getting enough exercise for their breed and age. However, not all tired dogs are always calm. In many cases it will help to tire your dog out so that they can relax at home. But with some dogs this is only half of the story ... they also need to learn that sometimes you want them to do ... absolutely nothing!

CURE

You have a dog who is hyperactive, and possibly obsessed with their ball. Your dog needs to learn how to switch off.

Things that can help:

- The Nothing Exercise.
- Removing your dog's ball or toys that they like to fetch in the house for limited periods. Put the toys away out of sight. If your dog continues to focus on the toys' location, stand in front of your dog with your back to the toy and use your energy to send your dog away.

- You might need to use a lead within the house to act as a consequence if your dog doesn't calm down, or move away from the toy. Put the lead on for a short period, use your disagreeing noise/give a gently tug to stop the behaviour, ask for a "sit" and stroke your dog when they are calm. Repeat. Lots of little chances to learn. **NOTE - Dogs who are very worked up might need you to take hold of their collar and give a gentle tug to achieve a sit.**
- Another consequence might be to remove the dog from the room for a few minutes, only let them back when they are calm. Repeat.

- Try having an **energy detox** for a few days ... whereby you basically ignore your dog unless they are calm. You are feeding your dog energy when you look at them and talk to them ... except perhaps if you use a boring neutral voice. Try being unemotional and calm, and only stroke them when they are calm. You can still give them lots of love and cuddles, but in a calmer way.

It's worth considering outside factors such as diet. A diet too high in protein can result in a dog with no outlet for all their energy and may result in hyperactivity.

Listed below is the appropriate amount of protein for different dogs:

- Young Puppy - 30% Protein
- Adolescent Dog Nearing Adulthood - 25% Protein
- Adult Dog Low Activity - 18% Protein
- Adult Dog Normal Activity - 20/21% Protein
- Adult Dog High Activity - 25-30% Protein

If you can afford them raw meat diets can be great, but just make sure they aren't too protein rich for non-working dogs. The really good raw food diets include bones, fruit and vegetables, not just meat. You might want to try adding rice to reduce the protein percentage.

TIP - The longest walk of the day is best given in the morning, this will help to drain excessive energy stored up over-night.

20. POOR RECALL

PREVENTION

It's best to start training from the first day you have your dog home ... and that includes with 8 week old puppies. The key is never to tell your dog off if they don't come to you, or teach your dog they can ignore you. But rather to communicate the message coming to you equals excitement and treats, and that ignoring you isn't an option (use a long lead to reinforce this). See CURE for recall training steps.

CURE

The following method is great for puppies to learn good recall and for older dogs to re-learn their recall.

RECALL TRAINING

I am only going to focus on whistle training as it has many advantages. These include that your **emotion isn't transferred** to your dog, it is better for **long distance recall** and also if you previously have had poor recall you can **start afresh** with a new tool. For those people who have previously used a whistle it might be a good idea to change sounds e.g. two fast blows instead of one.

I prefer whistles that I can hear, but obviously your whistle choice is up to you as an individual. You need your whistle to be on a lanyard around your neck to free up both hands.

STEP 1 - ASSOCIATION

Your dog needs to associate your whistle with coming back to you, not with continuing what they are doing and coming back when they choose.

ASSOCIATION EXERCISE

- Get a small treat ready in one hand, blow your whistle and immediately feed your dog the treat (within 2 seconds of making your sound). Repeat 5 times.
- Now get a few treats in your hand, and walk backwards with your dog following. Every few seconds blow your whistle and reward your dog with a treat. You are teaching your dog to move forwards towards you at the sound of the whistle.

STEP 2 - PRACTISE WHISTLE RECALL WITH NO DISTRACTIONS (DURATION ONE MONTH)

I would recommend you practise the following in an area with **no distractions** for approximately one month. Just imagine how many times your dog has ignored you, or for new puppies how many much more exciting things there are going to be out there. You need to put the work in to counter balance this. **Your dog needs time to develop a new habit of always coming to you.**

WHISTLE RECALL

- You are going to start calling your dog from 1 meter away.
- The sequence is as follows - wait for your dog to look at you … then **whistle**, **crouch down**, open your arms and get **excited**/give them a **treat** when they come to you. Ideally **praise** should last for about **10 seconds**.
- Next you need to add in one more element. Lure your dog in with a treat, **hold your dogs collar or harness under their chin**, only then does your dog get the **treat**.
- Gradually increase the distance you call your dog from, **always making sure they are looking at you or already moving towards you**.
- You can add an **additional** element of **excitement** in by whistling, then **running away** (with your back to your dog), before turning around and crouching down, arms open to welcome your dog.

TIP – Hold your dog's collar before rewarding them with the treat.

STEP 3 - LONG LEAD TRAINING WITH LOW LEVEL DISTRACTIONS (DURATION ONE MONTH)

An ideal place is to go to a park with other dog walkers around. You need a long training lead of approximately 3-4 meters in length, and a harness for your dog. N.B. The use of a collar and long lead can result in neck injuries.

Practise your recall as in Step 2 when your dog is looking at you, or already moving towards you. In addition add in recalls when your dog is distracted sniffing the ground, or not looking at you. **If they don't come you need to instantaneously reel them in with the training lead.** When they get to you reward them with a treat and 10 seconds of excited praise and fast stroking. Thus teaching your dog they can't ignore you.

STEP 4 - OFF LEAD TRAINING (DURATION LIFE LONG)

In order to have good recall you need to continue your dogs training for the rest of their lives. , and , **On every walk you need to be doing at least one catch and release, and always taking out treats.** This means your dog doesn't associate coming to you with being put back on the lead.

Simultaneously you need to teach your dog that they have to **check in more with you, and follow you**. Just like on the loose lead walking they need to be walking with you, but on a much larger scale. **You actually achieve this by not calling your dog!**

You need to always do catch and release training, but the rest of the time it is often better to just walk off without telling your dog - the majority of dogs will follow and start to check in more.

CHECKING IN EXERCISE

It is worth doing an exercise whereby you deliberately walk off and leave your dog without calling them to test if they will follow you. When they come ignore them and keep walking off and changing direction. This simple exercise will make your dog more aware of where you are and encourage them to check in more.

ADDITIONAL RECALL TOOLS

- **Walking off** and ignoring your dog can often be as effective for getting them to come as calling them.
- If you **crouch down** every time you call your dog this can be used as a recall signal in itself. **It can be seen from a long way off, and can negate teaching your dog they can ignore you if you whistle them.** For instance if your dog is playing with another dog and you think they might ignore you, try crouching down and not calling them. Many dogs will come over to see you and can then be rewarded.

- The **"wait"** or **"stay"** command can be useful for dogs who are reluctant to come those last few meters. This needs to be practised at home many times with no distractions before being used on the walk. The idea is when your dog is close to you you can hold up your hand and ask them to stay where they are (in a low, firm voice), so you can then go over to them and put the lead on. Like the catch and release this should be practised on every walk for a reward, whereby the collar is held but the lead isn't put on. This method can be good for independent breeds such as huskies.
- The **emergency stop** is a great command to teach your dog, but takes lots of steps and might get confusing if I try and explain it. For this command please watch the corresponding video to learn the technique.

WHAT TO DO IF YOUR DOG IGNORES YOU

Ideally you only want to be whistling one time for your dog to come. However, what happens when you have misjudged the situation and your dog ignores you? The worst thing to do is to panic and repeatedly blow the whistle whilst your dog continues to ignore you.

The best thing to do is to assess the situation and whether you need to go over to intervene, or if the situation is safe then you can make use of your **alternative recall tools**. Either to go nearer and crouch down, or just to walk (or run) off in the opposite direction (without calling your dog). By using these methods to recall your dog you have avoided over calling them and setting them up to fail.

When they do come you can continue to ignore them, or if they come right up to you bend down and give them a reward. You want to avoid being ANGRY, as this will discourage your dog from coming to you in the future.

REALISTIC RECALL EXPECTATIONS

Although you are going to be able to greatly improve your dogs recall, in reality it may never be 100%. There is an area of about 20-30 meters surrounding you whereby your dog is going to be more responsive to coming when you whistle, despite being distracted.

Outside this 20-30 meter area there are different grades of distraction as to whether your dog will respond to the whistle, and many dogs will differ even within this range.

Low Grade - **Sniffing** - Your dog should respond (harder for scent dogs).
Medium Grade - **Playing with other dogs** - Puppies might not respond, but older dogs should respond, especially if you are walking away from them.
High Grade - **Prey** - Most dogs once outside a 20-30 meter radius, and many dogs even within this radius will not respond if called, the excitement of the chase is simply too high.

GOLDEN RECALL RULE - Don't set your dog up to fail, or teach them to ignore you by calling them when you know they aren't going to come.

21. TOILET TRAINING

As all dogs are different, the amount of time it will take to toilet train your dog will vary.

TOP TIPS

- Every time your puppy goes in the right place - reward with lots of excited praise, and possibly a treat.
- Don't get ANGRY when you catch your puppy in the house ... this will just mean they will try to go without being caught! If you do catch them in the act remain calm, hold their collar and walk them outside whilst giving your chosen toilet command word. If they finish their business outside, end with lots of praise and possibly a treat.
- Take your puppy outside regularly, especially after eating, drinking or sleeping.

- Try using a pet odour remover inside that doesn't just mask the smell but eliminates it. Otherwise your puppy will keep on going in the house because it will smell right. If your pup does a stool inside, move it outside and leave it there for a day to associate the right area with the right smell.

22. CRATE TRAINING

It's natural for dogs to always want to be with their family. To be separated is an unnatural behaviour that needs to be learned. There are two different aspects to crate training - day and night crate training.

NIGHT TIME CRATE TRAINING

Not all puppies are suitable to crate train from the first night. If the breeder has already started the process you should be able to continue straight away, or maybe if you have a breed of dog not predisposed to separation anxiety.

However, if you have a puppy who has never been in a crate before, or a breed known for it's separation anxiety tendencies you might want to rethink your options. It might be easier for your puppy to spend their first night in an open pen or box with high sides next to your bed. They should be able to see you, and if necessary you can dangle your arm in to stroke and comfort them.

During the first few nights you might need to take your puppy out for toilet breaks if they wake during the night. If this happens quietly praise your puppy, before bringing them quietly back to the crate. Avoid night time cuddles and play which will stimulate your puppy.

Once your puppy is happy in the crate during the day, they can then progress to spending night times alone in their crate.

DAY TIME CRATE TRAINING

Even puppies who are easy to crate train at night might take slightly longer during the day. It's easier for your dog to slowly get used to the crate. Ideally your new dog should gradually get acclimatised to their crate in their own time.

ACCLIMATISATION PROCESS

- Leave the **door open**, and allow your dog to explore the crate by themselves.
- Throw **food** into the crate as positive reinforcement with the area.
- Once your dog is settled and relaxed with the crate, shut the door for a few seconds.
- Practise unemotionally leaving the room, and immediately returning to left your dog out.
- Gradually increase the time the door is closed, and try to time opening the door when your dog isn't making a noise.

Over time your dog will come to associate the crate with safety and with being calm. Be patient, it may take a few weeks to gradually get your dog used to their crate.

PART THREE

USEFUL COMMANDS

1. VOICE CONTROL

Your energy is transmitted in your voice.

A **deep**, rough voice for **command** words (I use a growly low pitched man like voice), and a **high** excited voice for **praise** (I utilise my squeaky high pitched girly voice, or some might prefer to make a squeaky/kissing sound).

A calm, confident monotone voice can help to reassure your dog but isn't essential - a non-emotional response from you to a stressful situation, and confident body language can be the best form of reassurance you can offer your dog.

Every person and dog are different so you need to find what works best for you.

When you are giving a voice command ... **less is more.** A single word followed by a pause is more effective than a repeated command which is being ignored.

CASE STUDY

A man I met was training his dog to be a gundog. Usually his dog listened to him very well, the exception being the few days after he had his tonsils out. Without his strong healthy energy or the use of his voice his dog was free to ignore him.

2. INTENTION

If you don't have confident intentions and believe your dog is going to do as you have asked ... then your dog will sense this. **Basically your dog can read your mind!** In order for your dog to execute a command successfully you need to have the conviction and belief that your dog will follow your instructions.

Confidence is something that is hard to teach, it needs to come from within and can be gained through experience.

Whilst obviously intention is not a learned command, the right intention needs to be behind any interaction with your dog .. including when you issue a command.

3. HAND-SIGNALS

These can help your dog learn not just the verbal command, but visually and can help in projecting your energy. A pointing finger can be used for "sit", a flat hand held out for "wait" or a wave away can aid a "go play". Also, when doing recall bending down with your arms out open wide can signal to your dog you wish them to return.

4. SIT

If you have mastered projecting your energy ... you can teach a "sit" without using treats. In an open area move towards your dog and point your finger, and say "sit" the instant they sit down. If you are bonded with your dog, your energy and intention should be enough to achieve this.

You can then use your excited energy as praise. Food rewards can also be used, and can be an additional reward in conjunction with your exuberant energy.

Alternatively, you can use a treat to lure your dog into a sitting position. Draw the food back over your dog's head and allow them to follow it with their nose to encourage them to sit. Lots of excited praise, and the treat should follow a successful "sit".

5. LEAVE IT

By claiming toys/objects from your dog from an early age (keeping them still and waiting until your dog walks away) you naturally teach your dog to leave it. In fact if you give the command "leave it" every time you take something from your dog, they will learn the command by association.

If your dog hasn't learned to "leave it" - you can teach it with food:

- Have a slightly open fist with a piece of food inside, and in your other hand a treat to actually give to your dog.
- Let your dog sniff the treat in your slightly open hand. Project your energy in a low growly voice saying "leave it" ... until they give space, look away or look at you and then immediately give them the treat from your other hand.

- Once they have got the hang of this you might want to progress to the floor, with your hand hovering over the treat and eventually your foot. Each time your dog moves away reward them with the other treat.

6. WAIT

Treats can be used as a reward, but as with any command this can also just be taught using your energy and excited praise.

NOTE - Always give the reward when you return to your dog and then release them, do not confuse your dog by getting a wait/stay and then doing a recall and giving a treat. Initially the two exercises need to be differentiated to foster full understanding in your dog's mind.

- Ask your dog to sit or lie down. Hold your hand out flat in front of you, and give the command "wait". You need to use a firm voice for the command.
- Move back a short distance ... only about 1 metre to start with. Keep your energy focused through your outstretched hand and arm. If your dog goes to move, instantly counter this with a disagreement in voice control and a quick movement of your hand.

- Your dog is holding their position. Initially don't make them wait long, go back immediately and get really excited!
- Slowly increase the distance and duration over time.

The "wait" command can be useful if you need to leave your dog for short periods. They will know you are coming back, and this should help reduce any short-term separation anxiety.

It can also be useful to rescue objects from your dog. Instead of chasing them and creating a fun game which your dog will love to repeat. It is useful to get them to "wait" first, whereby you then go over to your dog, before issuing the "leave it" command.

In addition the "wait" command can be used to get your dog back onto the lead. If you can ask them to "wait" in one place, you can then go over to them and hold their collar before placing the lead on them.

7. GO PLAY

To be able to send your dog away from you can be useful.

- Choose a command such as "go play" and say it initially as your dog is running away from you.
- Use a high excited voice to give the command.
- Use an arm gesture moving away from you to indicate your intention.

NOTE – It can also be useful to send your dog away if they are displaying unwanted behaviour such as eating something nasty, or barking at another dog. In this case you need to change your tone of voice to a low, growly command voice combined with an arm signal to move your dog on.

8. BED

It can be a very handy command to ask your dog to go and stay on their bed. For instance, if your dog is barking at something, jumping at a guest or just has muddy feet.

- Start by walking your dog to their bed with a lead or collar. You don't want to be dragging them there, but rather walking them calmly.
- Place them on the bed whilst giving your chosen command word "bed" or "on your bed".
- Stand back and throw treats onto the bed.
- If you want them to stay there use the "wait" command.
- Start with short "wait" times, building up slowly to longer time periods.
- Release your dog from their bed.

SUMMARY

Your projected energy needs to equal that of your dog if you want them to listen to you. It shouldn't be less (they can ignore you), and it shouldn't be greater which can induce fear and a lack of trust.

To **increase** your **projected energy** you can **lean in** towards your dog.

To **decrease** your **projected energy** you can **turn away** and crouch down (helpful with nervous dogs).

You need to have the right confident intentions, because it's almost as if **dogs can read our minds!**

You don't need to be more dominant than your dog, but you do need to be more patient. You need to follow through every time and achieve the behaviour you desire.

POSITIVE EMOTIONS THAT CAN HELP YOUR DOG

- CALM
- CONFIDENT
- EXCITED

NEGATIVE EMOTIONS THAT CAN PRODUCE UNWANTED BEHAVIOUR

- ANGER
- PITY
- EMBARRASSMENT
- FRUSTRATION
- ANXIETY
- GUILT
- FEAR

Dear Reader,

I hope you have found Communicate A Message - Transform Behaviour to be helpful.

I have written this book mainly for my clients to use as a reference, but if anyone else finds it useful and can avoid the stresses associated with miscommunication ... it will have been worth the many hours it took to write and self-publish this book.

Many thanks,

Nicky

Also Available on Amazon:

Choosing A Puppy: Identifying Puppy Personalities and Suitable Breeds (ebook only)

Puppy Parenting: Rasing A Non-Reactive Dog (ebook only)

DISCLAIMER

The techniques described in this book should only be tried at your and your dog's own risk. You need to be able to feel calm in all situations, always think about the safety of everybody involved ... including other people and dogs.

ACKNOWLEDGEMENTS

Thank you to my dad Tom, and friend Nik for their help with editing. Dad your help and corrections over the years firstly with schoolwork, then my dissertation, and now with my books has been invaluable.

Many thanks to my good friend Kirsty, and my daughter Leoni who both helped with the outdoor filming. Leoni and my son Josh also appeared in some of the videos.

Thanks to my mum for always being there for me. Final thanks go to my husband Niko who has supported me throughout this process, and encouraged me to follow my dreams in becoming the Yorkshire Dog Whisperer.

REFERENCES

- Livestock Guardian Dogs and their role in large predator conservation, Inside Ecology, 16th May 2018, Paul White
- Jamie Dutcher: The Hidden Life of Wolves - Nat Geo Live
- Wikipedia
- Train to Adopt – The Nothing Exercise

Cover Photo - Pexels.com

Communicate A Message - Transform Behaviour
Copyright - Nicola Nakalevu 2021

Self-published - 2021

Printed in Great Britain
by Amazon